SIN

IS NOT YOUR

PROBLEM!

"I can observe what you are doing, but I can
not tell why you are doing it"

Dr. Jerry A. Grillo, Jr.

**"For you, O Lord, will bless the righteous; with favor
you will surround him as with a shield." Psalm 5:12**

SPECIAL THANKS

I want to thank all those who have helped in proofing this book and making it possible to be published. People such as April Mercer, Dr. Emilio L. Niglio, and Diamond Press

Also want to acknowledge my wonderful family who puts up with all my craziness. To my wonderful wife Maryann you are a Godsend. My son, Jerry, and my daughter, Jordan, I love you beyond words.

To my parents I love you dearly.

To my spiritual father Dr. Mike Murdock, Every book is a product of what you spoke to me eight years ago. Thanks

To all my readers, thank you for reading what God has placed in my heart.

To My Lord and Savior Jesus, no life would be complete without you in it. Thanks for your sacrifice on the cross that paved the way for me.

SIN IS NOT YOUR PROBLEM
ISBN 0-9710967-9-1
Copyright 2005 by FZM PUBLISHING
P.O. Box 3707
Hickory, NC. 28603

TABLE OF CONTENT

Every man of God is a compilation of what he has heard and read through the years. I was inspired to write this manuscript through the pains of my own ministry. I have had people I have mentored and prayed for until I was sick of teaching and praying. Afterward, they still would fall right back into their sins.

I want to thank all the men and women of God who have affected my life through the years. I can testify that what you read in this book you've seen and heard through the years. My goal was to put together a book that would make some sense to those who struggle with sin and cannot seem to gain control of it.

There's a great book that most Christians haven't read. It's called *"Surrender"* by Arthur Burt. This book had a powerful impact on me and caused me to dig deeper into the subject of pride and sin. *"Surrender"* is the key source of my pursuit to write and explain in depth the power of real victory over sin.

Sin really doesn't have power…. sin really can't control you… The real problem that is killing you is what causes us to sin. This book *"Sin Is Not Your Problem"* is a teaching that will ignite you to become a better believer. Dr. Arthur Burt, I thank you for your work and life of dedication and ministry.

Dr. Jerry A. Grillo, Jr.

We have had our religious movements in times past. The faith movement, the salvation movement, the name it claim it movement, the prophecy movement and many others.

I believe that we are about to walk into a revival of the **FAVOR OF GOD,** and when favor comes it will absolutely **make no sense.** The greatest gift God gave us is **Favor!**

Favor is the mercy of God personified.

Favor is the umbilical cord to what God has for us.

Favor will be the ingredient that will cause us to fulfill our destiny.

Favor is something that we are allowed to walk in. Everyone has the potential to walk in the favor of God. However, everyone will not do what it takes to receive God's favor.

Favor is a decision. Salvation is free… Everything else will require something on your part. Everyone wants favor, but is unwilling to do what it takes to obtain favor.

Favor will make the devil pay!

Favor will cause you to walk in circles you aren't qualified to be in. Favor is the transfer of access.

Favor will have you driving a new car and someone else will be making the payment.

Money can't buy you **favor**... but **favor** can get you money.

Favor can change your medical report.

Favor will postpone the storm that was scheduled to destroy you.

Favor will promote you while others are trying to destroy you.

Favor will protect you.

A WORD OF CAUTION IS REQUIRED:

When we are seeking the Lord we need to be aware that we should seek the Lord for Who He is and not for what He can do for us. I'm a firm believer in the law of expectancy. I believe that we need to expect the Lord to bless us. I am not looking for His mighty acts when I seek the Lord. I am looking for His mighty hand of love, mercy and presence. In this we will find His hand of favor.

Let me put it in this terminology. Seek the Lord's left hand of Holiness and you will receive His right hand of favor.

I've been teaching and preaching six years on favor. I can honestly say that when you walk according to the precepts and by-laws of the Word of God you will begin to experience awesome favor. My first book on favor was titled "The Weather Forecast for your Future... Extreme F.O.G." In that book I wrote about what it means to walk in the F.O.G. (favor of God), and how to become the F.O.G

"Sin Is Not Your Problem" is my first book completely off the F.O.G. Series. However, you will still find the favor message all through this book.

Get ready to enter into the place where hell has no access and where demons fear to enter. I believe that throughout these pages there are keys that will take you into a spiritual understanding that will allow you to cross the threshold of areas where you've never been in your life. Psalms says that the Lord is my refuge! That refuge is a person! There is a place in that person and in that place there is a peace that produces a posture of victory. Get ready for God to place you in your position.

God is going to place you into a position of greatness and favor. When you are done reading this book you are going to understand how much authority you really do have and how weak sin really is.

Sin does not have dominion over you. You are going to win!

What is standing between you and your dream?

Bishop Jerry Grillo gets to the very matter in his book, *"Sin Is Not Your Problem."* He addresses all of the vices we commonly use as an excuse and shows us from the Word of God they are only the symptoms of deeper issues.

Inspirational and informative, this book will open your eyes to truths you have never seen before. You will be enlightened, challenged and confronted as you read every power-packed page.

This book is a must-read for every Christian, and especially every Pastor. It certainly deserves two thumbs up. I was astounded by the revelation Bishop presented and found hope as he showed me that we have victory and dominion over every area the enemy tries to use against us. He is truly an agent of truth to this generation.

This phenomenal book is another success from the pen of Bishop Grillo. His acclaimed Favor of God (F.O.G.) series has brought change to the body of Christ all over the nation and the world. I challenge you to absorb every word into your spirit man so that it will impact your life and change your destiny.

I count it a blessing and a privilege to call Bishop Grillo my friend. He has been a source of inspiration and encouragement to my life, and I know he will do the same for you. I am excited for you, as you are about to embark on a new path of revelation and truth.

Many thanks to Bishop Grillo for such a rich and challenging message... keep the courage to follow your God-given dreams and experience the full potential of God's plan for your life as you gain victory over those things that would try to hold you back.

God has designed you for the extraordinary life in Christ Jesus.

Dr. H. Michael Chitwood
"The Authority"

I have been in ministry for more than twenty years, and have developed questions that until now I was afraid to ask. I have watched things in the church and have often asked myself, "How could this be?" How can so many people come to church, get stirred by the Spirit of God, run to the altar and confess everything that has been holding them down. They may give up cigarettes, they may confess an addiction, and they may lay down fear or some other problem. Whether it is from past sins or present sins they lay them down, and yet within weeks of their confession they are right back in the same problem?

Some of these individuals never even make it through the end of that day before they are right back in their mess. I know that they were being sincere. I am sure that they really intended to change. The truth is, that some how we are missing the proper key to unlock complete deliverance.

This bothers me because I know that when people come to the Lord they come for the most part with a sincere heart...with the intention of being delivered... but it seems that they are never completely set free from what they were bound to.

What went wrong?
- Did they actually get delivered?
- Isn't God more powerful than their addictions or problems?
- Are they so bound to their sins that they couldn't

receive their deliverance?

- Does Satan have that much control over us that we can't even confess our deliverance and be set free?

Something must be wrong in today's church. I know that there are those who have nothing but great success in everything they do, but for us who have to live in the real world I personally would like some answers.

Are we so powerless that we can't even pray a simple prayer of agreement and believe for someone to be delivered? Are we so ineffective that no matter what we do the people we pray for are still bound?

If you're like me you have read about all kinds of moves of God and all kinds of testimonies of those who instantly received the healing hand of God in a certain situation. Why do the majority of us witness something totally different?

The events that stirred me to write this book didn't come through deep earnest prayer…The inspiration of this book came to me by the way of helping a brother in the Lord who was caught up in the web of lust. This brother ministered to people, he was a leader in my church, his family hung out with me and we even took trips together.

This man sang on my platform, prayed for my people and came to the altar not once but often. One day someone brings me information about this person that was unbelievable. This man was in all kind of sexual sins and perversions. He was selling pornography on the Internet;

He was having sexual relations with not just one woman, but about thirty different women. He was caught in bank fraud and had lied to just about everyone he knows.

Now, here I am a Man of God, preaching all over the nation, author of several books and I couldn't even discern what this man was doing. I felt unknowledgeable and questioned my call. **Where is the power of discernment?** I know there are men and women who possess this gift and immediately would have known this man was lying. Most of us have to ask the question: "Where is God when you need him to expose those who might destroy their marriages or our ministry?"

The Word declares that we are supposed to walk in victory, yet as Christians we sure seem to be full of sin and ungodliness. In the church arena we should have marital restoration, family deliverances, addiction free lifestyles and a since of joy on our faces. However, the opposite seems to be the reality.

I have come to the conclusion, in my ministry life at this time, that sin is not our problem. There must be something deeper that causes men to sin. I can pray for all kinds of problems. I am perplexed and confused when I pray for someone who keeps doing the same sin over and over again.

I have asked myself this question, "Am I not anointed enough to help these people who are trying to lay down a life of sin?" My answer is we have the authority to do a lot of things, but we haven't been given the authority to make choices for others. I can remember as a young man asking my parents for advice and then making my own decisions, sometimes in contrast to what they had advised me to do. Generation to generation we all have a tendency to have to find out for ourselves. Experience is the most costly and painful tutor there is. However, many of us cannot learn from the experience of others. There is, in effect, the same law at work when we can pray for people to discover the truth, but they have to find it for themselves.

Document Your Journey

_____
_____
_____
_____
_____
_____
_____
_____
_____
_____
_____
_____
_____
_____
_____
_____
_____
_____
_____
_____
_____
_____
_____
_____
_____
_____

CHAPTER ONE

SKIN DEEP DELIVERANCE

CAN WE PRAY AND SOMEONE BE DELIVERED?

The question is: "Can we pray for someone to be delivered?" If we can, what is the proper prayer, and if we can't then what do we do as Christians to help those who are bound to a sentence of torture and ignorance?

The dictionary states that "deliver" means: *"To set free or save from evil, danger, or restraint (i.e.) delivered from bondage."*

I'm not saying that someone can't be delivered, or at times hasn't been completely delivered, but can my prayers alone deliver someone?

Real deliverance has nothing to do with what I am praying. It has everything to do with the one who is seeking to be delivered. Those who are in bondage to something, whether it is addiction, lust, lying, anger, sexual sins or any other spiritual bondage, must make the necessary changes in their mindsets that will facilitate their freedom or deliverance. The responsibility to be freed is not placed on the one who is praying, but on the person who is seeking to be freed.

You have no responsibility to those who refuse your counsel.

I believe that we can't pray for someone to be delivered. Deliverance or spiritual freedom is not set on the responsibility of prayer or the intercessor. Responsibility for deliverance is on the shoulders of the seeker through mentorship and discipleship.

What we like to do as Christians is to find the road of least resistance, and then create spiritual traditions to make us feel that we have fulfilled our spiritual obligations.

We find very little evidence in the Word that Jesus ever prayed for someone to be freed. Jesus always responded to the hurts and bondage of others with the instructions of go and sin no more. Jesus changed those around him because He took the time to mentor and disciple them.

We are also going to have to take the time necessary, with those who are in bondage, to really help them be freed from their sins. There will be times when we will have to lay hands on the person who is bound and pray a prayer of faith in the process of helping them. The power of impartation, in agreement with the one who is seeking relief from bondages, creates a partnership of faith that the Word of God says will drive out the spirits that have attached to those who are in bondage.

Don't misunderstand me. I am not doing away with prayer. I am a firm believer that prayer is an important part of our walk with the Lord. However, I do fear that we have lost the true meaning of prayer. What is the true meaning of prayer? Is prayer the avenue where we seek to free others or the place where we seek to free ourselves? I believe that prayer is set up for us to become acquainted with God and his attributes. We should labor to hear His voice. I'm not implying we do away with intercessory prayer groups or prayer. This book is not about prayer and fasting. It is about discovering the true victory over sin.

If we can pray for someone to be delivered then why is it that most of the people we pray for do not receive their deliverance? We have made prayer a ritual for requests and petitions. We have lost the power of relationship. Prayer is for us to build a relationship with God. This is not a doctrine; this is my personal conviction. I am not trying to start some new doctrine on prayer or the ministry of deliverance. I'm just stating what I have observed in my 23 years of ministry. If anything, I'm seeking the answers to questions that have yet to be answered. I hope by the end of this book you and I will come to a deeper understanding of how to win over sin. If you are like me, you know someone who has tried and tried repeatedly to be set free. Every time we turn around in church to look for them they are once again doing what they have been trying not to do. I'm not trying to beat a dead horse or be repetitive. However, I am trying to drive in this thought. Is prayer for deliverance all we have to do to see someone set free?

We keep praying, but the many we pray for never seem to change. Instead of praying for deliverance, maybe we should pray that they be enlightened to what has them in bondage. Could it be what has them in bondage isn't sin but something deeper and stronger than the action of sin? Discovering the truth will cause the person to seek the necessary possibilities to be freed.

We need to have understanding. It seems that most people who are sitting in our churches today have little, if any, understanding to some simple basic Biblical truths. The people I've come in contact with are always looking for some new fad, sermon or preacher who can get them to their promise land quick and easy without any responsibilities. They want a new emotional high. Always looking for what can make them feel good. Get it now, get it fast and don't wait for anything.

We've become church addicts. The only difference between a drug addict and a church addict is the use of drugs. What are they addicted to? **Emotional spiritualism**! If someone is made to feel bad in a church, they become convicted or are forced to face the truth about what they are going through then they will determine if they are in the right church or not. Men of God have been forced to water down the basic truths on change and absolute. They've been forced to preach fluffed up sermons hoping they made the majority of the congregation feel good and safe. If not they fear that they will be asked to leave. I'm not opposed to affirmation. I'm not against preaching in ways that encourage people not to quit or break focus to their dreams and visions. However, sometimes the truth is going to cut and require change! We need to understand that conviction is not condemnation.

Many people are becoming offended and wounded these days and it has caused us to birth a church with no stamina, no endurance and no power. There are people in our churches shouting praises while they are still living with, and having relations with, someone they are not even married to. What ever happened to services where people changed their lifestyle? These people are not even convicted about their sin. They come to church every week and most of them never even feel bad for their sins. Is it because they sense no unction from the pulpit and no anointing that allows them to face their transgression, which would cause them to desire change? These people just keep sitting in their mess, shouting praise and lifting up dirty hands believing that they are okay. What a mess. I fear for any spiritual leader who does not lay down some absolute truths about what is right and wrong. We need to set up some spiritual structure again. There needs to be some order in the house!

We have people lying, cheating, stealing and sowing

discord and they never feel one ounce of conviction. Why? The reason is we scream out grace and prosperity and never challenge people to change. Prosperity before our love for God is deadly. Before we seek the blessing let's get to know the one who is doing the blessing!

Bishop Charles Gore wrote in his book, **"Order and Unity,"**

"...The whole method of Christ, based upon His profound perception of the ultimate power of the true spiritual idea, conveyed as a message from God and apprehended by the single mind, has often been quite forgotten by the church.

Popular religions of all kinds have commonly been popular because they consisted in religious customs and rites, which were familiar and involved no mental effort, but let the minds and ideas of the people alone... The church has fallen into the habit of the world, and suffered men to enter the church and adopt its rites and ceremonies, with their minds, their ideas, almost untouched. Religion has been made easy, and its lifting power correspondingly lost, by neglect of the principle of Christ that only spiritual truth really apprehended is redemptive: that the will and heart cannot be rightly trained while no claim is made upon the mind, to change and deepen and elevate its ideas...

The penetrating demand of the truth is sacrificed to

popular adhesion, and today there is a cheap philanthropic (taken lightly) gospel, unaccompanied by any careful or exacting doctrine about God and sin and redemption, which plays a great part in popular Protestantism in England and America..."

Jesus saw the same sickness creeping into mainstream religion during His time. Jesus saw that the teachers of His day were indifferent and even hostile to the truth.

Again Bishop Gore states: *"Jesus pressed upon men with authority the searching spiritual claim of the truth. He made them feel that enlightenment of mind, change of ideas, is the first necessity of spiritual progress, and that redemption is by spiritual knowledge."*

Even in the early 1900's we can see this cheap weak gospel being preached. It is the same today. We are building mega churches, but are we really building mega people who are the manifestation of Christ. When we put no demand on the minds of our people to line up and change we do them an injustice. We give them a feel good sermon and most of those who leave never go to church again. Why? They see our weak convictions and powerless churches. What is their example or more importantly; who is their example?

We have all witnessed this degradation in the church if we would be honest with each other and ourselves. What do we do? We have them come forward, pray some simple prayer, call them delivered and let them leave

21

feeling delivered. We never touch the real problem, and that problem is not the devil or a demon. The real problem is the unwillingness **to change.**

The whole reason people become bound and tormented in their lives is the result of their **decisions**. The real enemy we fight is not called the devil, Satan or Lucifer...no the real enemy is **bad decisions**. Dr. Mike Murdock said to me one day, *"Decisions decide your wealth."* Now change one word; decisions decide your joy, and decisions decide your relationships. We need to realize that if we are going through something that is hard, it might be the consequence of a bad decision.

When we find someone who has made a bad decision, we must let him or her walk through the consequences of that bad decision. If we don't, then how will **anyone learn**? Consequences are the best instructor for fixing bad decisions. Pain is a great teacher. A child can be told many times not to touch the hot stove surface while the stove is on. That child may not quite get the meaning to the message because of the lack of pain or consequences. Let that child touch the hot surface and there will be no more need for instructions. Why? Experience though pain has taught them the meaning to the message. **Pain is a motivator.**

> **CONSEQUENCES ARE THE BEST TEACHER FOR BAD DECISIONS**

My mentor, Dr. Murdock, says

it with such power. He says, "Experience is the most costly tuition, and mentorship is the cheapest way to learn." Unfortunately, most people learn by experience. Maybe the reason why is the result of pride. Pride causes people not to respect what others know. We can't stand it when others seem to know more than we do, so we must find out for ourselves, and the result is called experience. Now, this principle doesn't apply to everyone and to every situation, but it does apply more than we would like to admit. Think about it, maybe we could solve a lot of our spiritual problems if we quit blaming everything on the devil. Just a thought! Most Christians I talk to put more emphasis on the enemy than they do on the Lord. We are constantly talking about bad things and wrong relationships. We lift up the works of what we do wrong in our voices. What if we spent more time speaking about those things that are godly and wholesome? When we are experiencing crisis, and we know deep down that it was or is the result of a decision we made, we have to face it, learn from it and move on. We learn by two senses... pain or pleasure. Pleasure moments teach us, but for some reason the lessons learned do not last. Pain moments usually last a lifetime. Prosperity is a great teacher... adversity is even greater.

> **PAIN IS NECESSARY**

Pain is not necessarily a bad thing; pain can serve us and help us work through to our promotions.

PAIN IS A MOTIVATOR...

When we are having pain in our bodies it forces us to seek help from those who are qualified to help us. I've heard stories of those who went to the doctor as a result of pain, and they would have died in the night if they had not gone to the doctor. The pain they were experiencing motivated them to seek greater wisdom, and that resulted in them living and not dying.

PAIN FORCES CHANGE...

When we begin to do things that are harmful to our bodies it cries out, and the message is usually sent in aches and pains. When we hurt long enough we begin to seek the avenues of change. How many times have the pains around you caused you to stop long enough to evaluate what's causing your pain; and when you discover it you changed what was hurting you? Pain can force change.

PAIN INFORMS US TO WHAT IS NOT WORKING...

Pain is information. For instance, I enjoy working out and I'm every athletic. Every year our church plays this football game we now call the **"TURKEY BOWL."** This football game is played every New Years Day. This last game, 22 men and teenagers gathered on the field ready to take on their opponents and win. We were all ready to experience the thrill of victory or the agony of defeat.

This game lasted four hours and within two hours of playing I began to feel pain all over my body, especially in my left knee. What did I do? I'll tell you. I began to take the information in. I began to realize that a 42-year-old man cannot play ball like my thirteen-year-old son. I started processing the information the pain was sending to my brain. That information was letting me know that if I kept playing at that level, I was going to pay dearly for it. *So what did I do?* I slowed down and paced myself. My pain gave me vital information and I responded accordingly.

What if I began to rebuke my pain, and stood on the promise of God's word that we walk in divine health? Would that have kept me from suffering the consequences of my decision? **NO, IT WOULD NOT!** There are some things that are just plain common sense. If we persist on ignoring the pain we will pay dearly for it. So pain is not always a bad thing. If I take some type of substance, say for instance, some kind of pain reliever so that I can ignore what my body is trying to tell me, would this benefit me in the long run? No, it would not! Oh, for the moment I would be able to function, but in the end, the pain that was warning me to slow down will now be the pain that causes my punishment for ignoring its instructions. Pain is warning me that there is about to be a structural overload and the consequences are about to be out of my control. **I must stop or I will pay.**
Pain is not hurting me for no reason. Pain is informing me of a problem. The same is true in life. Sometimes the pains of the past are trying to teach you not to repeat the same decision in your present. Don't let valuable information pass you by just because you are afraid to

inspect the discomfort of pain in your life.

Looking at our mistakes and learning from them can help us not to repeat them. However, ignoring them causes the life of mistakes to be relived over and over again. This is why a woman who has lived in a battered relationship, will eventual leave the man who has beaten her... **and what will she do?** She will walk right back into the same problem with a different man. Why? She wouldn't face her discomfort and learn from her pain. Refusal to listen to the pain of consequences can be very costly. Haven't you ever noticed people who can't seem to get over what's been destroying them? What you are unwilling to face you can never fix. What you refuse to see will eventually kill you. Until you know where you are, you will never be able to chart the course to where you want to be.

SIN SHALL NOT HAVE DOMINION!

"Likewise you also, reckon yourselves to be dead indeed to sin, but alive to God in Christ Jesus our Lord. Therefore do not let sin reign in your mortal body, that you should obey it in its lusts. And do not present your members as instruments of unrighteousness to sin, but present yourselves to God as being alive from the dead, and your members as instruments of righteousness to God. For sin shall not have dominion over you, for you are not under law but under grace."
Romans 6:11-14 NKJV

We cannot move into this book any further until we have the same understanding of some word meanings.

WHAT IS SIN?

Sin has been defined as many things.

In the 1800's we had the inquisitions and the investigations. Everybody in the church leadership went on witch-hunts. You were considered to be possessed if you didn't act according to the opinion of others. People were arrested and tried in what were called witch trials when they acted strange or out of the norm. Usually when someone was taken to trial they were convicted as being of the devil. This would incur the penalty of being drowned or burned. When these so- called demon possessed people were tortured, it was believed that this would drive out the evil spirit thus freeing the witch or warlock from the influence of the evil spirit. How convenient it was just to accuse some one and then do away with them without ever having to take the time necessary to help them. What a messed up system that was. This is what I call looking for demons under every bush. *I don't believe that there are demons under every bush, but I do believe that there are demons under some bushes.*

Religion was very stringent on what you could and could not do in the early part of the twentieth century. They used phrases like: Walk holy... Live holy... Don't do anything to mess up your walk with the Lord. The church became rule oriented. Man began to establish holiness with the way you dressed, talked, ate, drank and acted.

The leaders of the church set up watchers to tell on those who didn't live up to the rule. They made sure that every Christian was miserable. I am not bashing where we came from. However, I am concerned that we have taken our walk with the Lord a lot less serious than those who have been before us. I wish that we could come to some middle ground on the understanding of walking with the Lord.

Let me interject that it was never God's plan for us to separate or to walk away from something...a bad habit, wrong attitudes, substances abuse, spirit of anger, etc. No one can really walk away from their desires or problems, without some understanding of what they are walking into. Try to change your focus instead of

CHANGE YOUR HABITS... CHANGE YOUR LIFESTYLE

trying to change your walk and your sin lifestyle. What you focus on you will eventually become. What has your attention is mastering you. Trying to walk away from actions that you have been doing for years is almost impossible. **Change your habits and you will change your lifestyle.**

LAW OF DISPLACEMENT:

You don't focus on the darkness if you want to expel the darkness in a room. You don't have to work up your faith or confess that the darkness is gone. What you do is go and flip the light switch on, and the entry of the light forces the darkness to exit.

Quit crying about it… and start doing things different today. We need to seek to grow closer to the Lord. God had to prepare the children of Israel for a new way of living when He brought them out of Egypt. Allowing them the time to go through the wilderness did this. God had to adjust them from a welfare mentality to a warfare mentality in the desert. God had to take out an entire generation to get His plan fulfilled. God changed their focus to what they were becoming and not on what they were. It was a new mentality of possessing and not being possessed; not a spirit of moving from but moving to something greater than where they had been. The difference between a burden and a blessing is possession!

When I was a youth pastor young people would come to me and say, "Pastor Jerry, I have this sin or that sin, how can I come to God with all these problems?" My reply was, **"Come as you are."** God will take you as messed up and dirty as you can come. When you start entering into God's presence… He will begin to clean you up. **Just come!**

- Come as you are…
  - Come addicted…
    - Come hurting…
      - Come angry…

Reminds me of the old Hymn; *"There's room at the cross for you, though millions have come there's still room for one…"*

Whatever you have done or are doing, just make sure that you don't ignore God's leading. Take that step of change and come to Jesus. We need to renew our passion for the name of Jesus. It seems that we have become enamored with so many teachings; Faith, Prosperity, Healing, Confession, Motivation, Favor... What we need to focus on is the Name of Jesus. Jesus said if we would lift Him higher He would draw all men unto Him. Maybe our churches aren't growing the way we would like them too... Could it be our focus is on everything but the right thing? God said build up my name; I'll build your church. If the Lord doesn't build the house the laborers labor in vain.

God's complete plan is for you to be free from the control of sin and to have a clean life... I do believe we can live such a life. We are not to separate from Him but to separate to Him! We are not to separate from sin...but separate unto Jesus! The closer you get to him the less you will sin. Sin is an acronym for <u>S</u>TOP <u>I</u>T <u>N</u>OW! Stop running away from your weakness and start running to the Lord.

S. I. N.
STOP IT NOW!

What is sin? It is **DISOBEDIENCE**! That's it; no great thesis or phrase, just one word. Sin is disobedience to an instruction from God. It doesn't matter whether that instruction comes from the Bible, or from your parents, or from your spiritual leaders. If the Word of God can back the instruction, and you disobey, you have at that moment sinned. Sin exists from the gutter… to the pulpit. The bible declares that sin is "lawlessness." *"Whoever commits sin also commits lawlessness, and sin is lawlessness…" 1 John 3:4 NKJV*

The Greek word for "lawlessness" is *"anomia,"* which means, "the condition of being without law, because of ignorance of it or because of violating it." Lawlessness means not submitting to the laws or authority of God. Sin is the consequence of something much deeper in us. What causes me to want to break God's laws and submit to something else?

The author R.C. Sproul says: "YOU CAN HAVE NO SOUND THEOLOGY, WITHOUT SOUND DEMONOLGY."

How does sin become the result of what causes consequences in my life? What causes us to sin? The truth is that we sin because something in us is driving us to sin. I don't believe that people by the majority live to sin. I do not in any way believe that people want to sin or that they study and strive to be sinners. There is a greater force in us that drives us to sin. Sin is not the cause but the consequence of the cause. Sin is not the problem. Sin has no power over us and by the scripture we just read... Sin shall not have dominion over you. Sin shall not rule us. We should be ruling sin.

Sin is disobedience.

Anything you do contrary to what God has said to do is sin. Sin is the cobweb, not the spider or the problem. Sin is the consequences of something greater and deeper in all of us. There is something much greater in us that causes us to sin. However, I'm not ready to dive into the discovery of the spider just yet. We need to gain some greater revelation on some basic rules before we can move into and discover what the spider is.

"Sin shall not have dominion over you." **Sin shall not rule our domain**

What is dominion? *TO RULE IN YOUR DOMAIN!*

In *Romans 6*, the word "dominion" in the Greek is "Kurios", which means supremacy or supreme in authority (i.e. controller.)

Sin shall not have supremacy over you... sin shall not control you. It's not that we aren't going to sin; it's that we are not controlled by sin. We must first stop sin's control over us in order to be free from the bondage of sin. Do we have to keep on doing what we know is wrong? Does sin have that much dominion over us? This would make **Romans 6:14** wrong. I believe that once we discover what's causing us to sin we will stop building our lives around the consequences of sin.

To rule is to dominate an area in which we are ruling. To dominate is to rule or control by superior power. We must understand that we have been given some power to rule and to dominate this earth. I know that the popular persuasion is that when the first Adam in Genesis fell he gave up the earth to Satan, and now Satan owns the right to dominate rule and control. I do not give into this persuasion because God never gave Adam the earth. He only gave him dominion to rule while He was not present.

"The earth is the Lord's, and the fullness thereof; the world, and they that dwell therein. For he hath founded it upon the seas, and established it upon the floods." Psalm 24:1-2 KJV

The earth is the Lord's and the fullness thereof, the world, and they that dwell therein. God never relinquished the earth nor did He ever give control of the earth to Adam. If God never gave Adam control, then we must also assume that Satan never gained control either. Adam had nothing to release or to let go of. He wasn't the owner, he was just being allowed to rule while God was not present. The power of withstanding from the curse of sin is first to let go of complete control.

When we understand that God is:
- All-powerful, (omnipotent)
- All knowing and (omniscient)
- Present everywhere at all times... (Omnipresent)

...we will let go of control. Adam ruled until God showed up then Adam would bow. He would worship God and in his worship would give God his

> **"Worship creates focus"**

proper place; **DOMINION.** Adam would maintain his focus. His focus wasn't to rule over Eden but to worship almighty God. Real worship is un-rehearsed. Real worship comes from the heart and not from the song leader or church choir. Worship prepares us for God's blessings. It changes our focus from ourselves to God. Worship is the ability to bow and promote whom we are really connected to. Worship allows us the avenue to find comfort and access into God's presence.

You see the truth is that Eden wasn't created for Adam, it was created for God. Eden was a place carved out on the earth where God could dwell in communion with whomever He desired to allow in to his garden. Adam wasn't the ruler of Eden. Adam was only allowed to control the earth while God was absent from Eden. Eden's atmosphere was conducive for God to enter it. It was God's place, and as long as man walked according to His instructions he could walk freely in God's

SIN SHALL NOT HAVE DOMINION

atmosphere. Have you created an atmosphere where God wants to dwell?

The ability for Adam to let God have dominion over him gave him the ability to have dominion. The spirit of humility is to give God his proper place, which places you in proper order and position. The proper position is dominion and not a position to be dominated by anything or anyone but God. We become arrogant and self-centered when we lack the humility to relinquish our kingdom for God's kingdom When we allow God his proper place he begins to allow us ours.

THE GREAT QUESTION:

Lucifer saw man, and man's relationship with God, and he was jealous. After all, Lucifer was the best God could do without making him God. Lucifer, which means "light bearer," was the light carrier of God. He brought all of heaven to worship and then carried that worship to God. One day, Lucifer began to look at himself. He saw his flawlessness, and he began to receive worship unto himself. Lucifer was found holding back some for himself when he brought God His rightful worship. This is one of the reasons the tithe needs to be paid. Don't be caught holding what rightfully belongs to God. He became self-conscious instead of God-conscious. Lucifer was defeated the moment he had the thought to keep what was rightfully God's.

I'm not of those who believe that there was a long drawn

out war in heaven between Lucifer and his angels and God and His angels. I believe the moment God became displeased with Lucifer, Lucifer was forbid to experience God's atmosphere, and was sentenced for eternity to stay out of the presence of God. Satan is now cast down to the earth where he can dwell without the power to be forgiven. We must have a clear understanding that Lucifer must have ruled on the earth before Adam was ever created.

Eden wasn't created for Adam. Eden wasn't created for Lucifer. Eden was created for God to have a place where He could come to earth and walk or dwell among his creation. Lucifer was in Eden before man was… possibly before he even fell. *"Thou hast been in Eden the garden of God…"Ezekiel 28:13 KJV*

In Luke Chapter 10, Jesus tells us that all authority is given unto him… That He saw Satan cast out of heaven like a lighting bolt… Some time before *Genesis Chapter 1:-2,* all this took place. Dr. Kelly Varner says, *"Once upon a time when there was no time, in a place called nowhere on the back side of nothing there was a meeting. Present in that meeting was God the Father, God the Son, God the Holy Spirit and you. Lucifer had already been cast out, the Lamb had already been slain, resurrected and was sitting at the right hand of the Father."* We know that in **Ephesians** Paul states that we were made before the foundations of the earth: *"Just as He chose us in Him before the foundation of the world,* *that we should be holy and without blame before Him in love..." Ephesians 1:4 NKJV*

Think for a moment. This pristine, picture perfect God whose only obsession is order, *order is the accurate arrangement of things,* has a world sitting out in space... full of darkness, void and nothing on the earth is complete. Just floating there, sticking out like a sore thumb. How long had the earth been in that state? Only God knows how long. No one in heaven would dare to mention or talk about it. (***Genesis Chapter 1***)

Imagine the surprise of all the angels and demons when all of a sudden the spirit of the Lord starts hovering over the face of the deep. Notice, that the spirit is always in the place set up where the Lord is about to speak up. The Holy Spirit knows the thoughts of God. Now God speaks over the earth and declares "LET THERE BE..."and there it was. We should always speak after the spirit moves. Don't just stop and wait for someone to preach when praise and worship is over in your services. Take some time to speak.
- Speak over your life.
- Speak over your children.
- Speak over your finances and let the atmosphere be permeated with your faith.

God decided to move from where He was to being present on the earth after He had spoken all things into existence. Here is where I get "goose bumps." God starts to play with dirt until he finds an image he likes. Everything on the earth, and in the earth, God spoke and there it was. He didn't need to do anything but speak. *Hebrews 11* declares that we know that the Word of God framed the worlds. God said, "Let there be light!" and there was light, and it stayed where it was told to stay and hasn't moved. When God speaks... His word is everlasting to everlasting. Then it's time for God to do something that is definitely contrary to what God has ever done to this point. God decides not to speak man into existence but to come down and touch man. God forms man by moving dirt around until He is satisfied with an image. Then he exhales so that man can inhale. God breathes into man and man becomes a living being. When God exhaled, the spirit of God entered into man. Blood began to flow through man's flesh. The Word declares that life is in the blood.

All the habitants of the earth and heaven stood in amazement. Lucifer, Gabriel and Michael are all watching as God steps out of character. This God, the creator of all things, reaches out and touches dirt? Then he does something that absolutely takes all of heavens breath away. God begins to reach for a gift to give this creature called man. God is going to crown man, and what does He crown him with... not a crown of gold, not a crown of silver, nor pearls or emeralds. He looks all over and begins to ponder, "What is the best I have to put on this flawed creature?" God crowns him with His **GLORY!**

What do you think heaven thought when all this time they have all secretly longed for that touch? Man was the only thing that ever received God's touch. The truth for today, is that man has been in need of a touch from God ever since.

Giving man a piece of God's Glory must have sent Lucifer into a frenzy. After all, wasn't that what Lucifer was longing for, to grab hold of the Glory of God? Now, here God is giving this precious gift not to a perfect creature like Lucifer, Michael or Gabriel, God is giving it to this flawed, imperfect creature called MAN!

Lucifer must have stared for days at this creature, trying to figure out what it was about Adam that drove God to come everyday and walk with him and talk with him. Lucifer is about to go mad... He can't figure this one out...what is this flawed and weak creature that has God's attention like no other creature? So here comes **Psalm 8**, the question that must have put heaven in absolute silence while all of the angelic hosts are waiting for God's answer. **What is a MAN...?**

"What is man that you are mindful of him, and the son of man that you visit him? For you have made him a little lower than the angels, and you have crowned him with glory and honor." Psalm 8:4-5 NKJV

"LORD, what is man, that you take knowledge of him? Or the son of man, that you are mindful of him?" Psalm 144:3 NKJV

After all this drama, God speaks to man and blesses Adam, and then gives him complete and total power or dominion over God's affairs. *"And God blessed them, and God said unto them, Be fruitful, and multiply, and replenish the earth, and subdue it: and have dominion over the fish of the sea, and over the fowl of the air, and over every living thing that moved upon the earth." Genesis 1:28 KJV*

The Hebrew word for dominion is: "Radah" (raw-daw'); *a primitive root; to tread down, i.e. subjugate; specifically, to crumble off.*
Copyright (c) 1994, Biblesoft and International Bible Translators, Inc.)

Sin shall not have rule or dominion over you. Sin shall not tread you down. Sin shall not cause you to crumble or be broken off the whole anymore. God has made provision for the penalty of sin. However, we are still not where we need to be. We must keep searching for the cause; to discover the cause can fix the consequences. Life is made up of cause and effect. Sir Isaac Newton's law applies here as well.

DOCUMENT YOUR JOURNEY

CHAPTER THREE

THE LAW OF CAUSE AND EFFECT

Let's review what we should already know. The universe is formed according to laws. Each law is in perfect harmony with each other and a lesser law will always give place to a greater law. How do these laws stay in complete agreement? When someone or something submits to the principles of one law that law has a precedent to take over.

We know that the law of Aerodynamics has existed since the beginning of time, yet for thousands of years men who even thought of such things were considered crazy or possessed by evil spirits. One hundred years ago man could not fly, but man found out early in this century that flight is possible.

What if you and I were standing on a building and I told you that I could fly if I jumped off the building. You would most likely say to me, "No you can't." If I asked you, "Can men fly?" You would have to answer yes. Well, then, I will jump from this roof and fly. You said that men could fly. I know, before I jump, I'll pray, believe and confess that I can fly, and when I have adequately covered my spiritual obligation I will jump off this roof and fly. HERE I GO... I'M JUMPING... I'M HOLDING OUT MY ARMS.... I'M FLAPPING THEM... OH NO, I'M FALLING! BOOM! The asphalt and I are now one. My face is bleeding, my body is aching and my head is splitting. I guess man really can't fly. What went wrong?

- I prayed
- I confessed
- I believed

But I did not fly!

TRUE IS NOT ALWAYS TRUTH...

True: man can fly. *Truth*: only if he submits to the law of aerodynamics. Let me clarify for a moment. Satan loves to use this powerful weapon of deception. He loves to tell you what's true, and in telling you what's true, never gives you the truth.

Favor Key "Revelation without wisdom is divisive."

The only absolute truth is Jesus. The book of Revelation tells us that there is a bottomless pit created for Satan and his followers. Anything that isn't built on the proper foundation, and that foundation is Christ, is bottomless. Truth must have the promotion of Jesus in it. Jesus said they should know the truth, and the truth that they know shall set them free. *(John 8:32)* We like to make this all spiritual and it's not. Yes, we must discover the truth and confess that Jesus is Lord. Yes, we must submit to a life of daily commitment to his Word. Every truth and principle discovered will unlock another level to your promotion. When we gain understanding of a truth, we can walk in that understanding, and use that truth or principle to unlock what were once closed doors. Wisdom is the principle thing above all else gain understanding. *(Proverbs 4:7)*

Remember, we're talking about true versus truth. Man can fly, yet there must be more to the equation. The truth is man can only fly when he submits to the law of **"Aerodynamics."** I don't care how much you pray... study... fast... praise... or confess. You are not going to fly anywhere until you activate the law of aerodynamics. Gravity will have to let you go when you do. Gravity has power over you until the greater law of aerodynamics is activated.

Law means "rule of action." There are universal laws and there are spiritual laws. They both work on the power of cause and effect.

FOUR LAWS
1. <u>PRINCIPLE LAWS</u>: Principle Laws mean that each event that occurs may be observed according to the principles that operate to bring it about. We can extract from things simply by submitting to the law of principles. The Dictionary defines

45

principles as, a fundamental truth, law, doctrine, or motivating force, upon which others are based. A rule of conduct... The ultimate source, origin, or cause of something...

2. <u>UNIVERSAL LAWS</u>: Universal Laws do not operate in only part of our lives, or inconsistently with our lives. Laws are constant and operate in every situation the same way, in every place within the created universe, at each level of consciousness.

3. <u>KNOWABLE LAWS</u>: Knowable Laws are more than words we use to describe it. We can understand it by its operation in our life. We can create a mental model of the principle and how it works, and use the model to predict the consequences of any proposed decision.

4. <u>USEABLE LAWS</u>: We can act according to our own understanding of the law, and apply the principle in any given situation. We have the ability to place the law into motion through idea, emotion and physical action.

We use the law of cause and effect by creating a desire, following through that desire using thought, word or deed and then experience the consequences.

The great astronomer and mathematician, Galileo,

believed that nature works according to mathematical laws, and observations of nature are explained when we find the relational mathematical law. We must be quite specific in what we mean by a scientific law, so as to distinguish it from a physical concept or scientific theory. Sir Isaac Newton published a paper entitled _The Mathematical Principles of Natural Philosophy_ commonly known as _The Principia,_ in 1687. Newton's discovery was that there are four rules of reasoning. These rules were to guide scientist in scientific process.

First rule: **PRINCIPLE OF PARSIMONY**
Scientist should make no more assumptions or assume no more causes that are absolutely necessary to explain their observations.

Second rule: **PRINCIPLES OF CAUSE AND EFFECT**
The belief that what occurs in nature is the result of cause and effect relationships, and where similar effects are seen then the same cause must be operating.

Third rule: **PRINCIPLES OF UNIVERSAL QUALITIES**

The belief that those qualities, such as mass or length, which describe bodies exposed to our immediate experience also describe bodies removed from our immediate experience, such as stars and galaxies.

Fourth rule: **PRINCIPLE OF INDUCTION**
Induction is the process of deriving conclusions about a class of objects examining few of them and then reasoning for the particular to the more general (deduction is the process of reasoning from the general to the more specific.)

I mention all this to address that maybe we blame too much of our problems on Satan and not enough on our own actions. We are trying to fight sin, and we must come to the understanding that sin is not the cause of my actions but the consequences of them. Life is made up of trade offs. Every decision has effects to them. Your decision (cause) creates consequences (effects) in your life, good or bad.

How many times do we blame so much of our problems on the spiritual realm when it had nothing to do with heaven or hell, but had everything to do with our decision? Someone once told me that if I were in doubt don't do it. Don't make a decision if you can't feel good about it. Take some time to gather more information so that you won't have to face the consequences if it's a bad decision. The proof that we make bad decisions is debt. Most of us are in so much financial debt, only to discover that after we purchased what we thought we needed so badly, wasn't what we really needed at all.

There are universal laws and spiritual laws. Unlocking them causes the reaction needed to grow.

GOD NEVER GAVE YOU THE KINGDOM:

For instance, I hear people all the time in churches make statements that are unscriptural. They only make them because they heard someone else say them. Tradition has ruined more Christians than Satan. Statements like, "God has given me the kingdom; therefore, I will not be in poverty," yet that is not true. Nowhere in the bible do we read that God gave the kingdom to men. However, we do read that God gave the kingdom to Jesus. Let me first show you the verse so you can see the truth.

" And I will give you the keys of the kingdom of heaven, and whatever you bind on earth will be bound in heaven, and whatever you loose on earth will be loosed in heaven." Mathew 16:19-20 NKJV

Jesus didn't give us the kingdom, but He did give us the keys to the kingdom... the power to shut and open doors in our life.

Everything you will ever need to fulfill your destiny already exists in you. When God created the earth He put everything that would ever be in the earth. God created everything out of the one. He didn't have to speak but once, and in that one spoken sentence everything that needed to be was. Out of the one thing, God made everything. This is so powerful; if you take hold of this revelation you will begin to understand why the enemy hates you so much, and why you should believe in you.

Let's examine this truth!

People are going to have to grasp the truth that they will only change as <u>they</u>, not someone else, <u>desire</u> <u>to</u> <u>change.</u> Desire is not enough! To make the change effective and lasting... transition must take place. Transition is the valley between what you are and what you want to change into. The inability to cross the valley of transition will cause you to only want to change but never allow you the power to change. Change must move in the force of transition. Most people who start the steps of change never do change because they begin to fear the valley of transition. Stay with me, we're going somewhere!

Transition is a passing from one condition, form, stage, activity, place, etc. to another *b*) the period of such passing...to modulate.
©1995 Zane Publishing, Inc. ©1994, 1991, 1988 Simon & Schuster, Inc.

To make transition, which will eventually facilitate change, you must end to begin. To begin something you must end something. Change is the easy decision. It's transition that's going to take every bit of your will power to make. You can't even begin to make transition until you first decide to end what's been keeping you from change. If you desire to quit smoking, or to stop a bad habit, you must first have an end date so you can have a beginning date. This is where the power of prayer is needed. Now, you should pray for discernment and pursue the Word of God for deeper connection to the SIN

Holy Spirit. He is the only person who can speak to the real you.

OUT OF THE ONE CAME THE MANY:

The power to change and quit sinning is not coming from your pastor… it's not coming from heaven… it's not coming from a counselor or your friends. It is coming from within you. You have the power with God's help to overcome any sin. The principles have always been within you and around you. These laws that govern us are God given and established laws. Sir Isaac Newton, or any other scientist or philosopher, didn't think them up or create them out of their minds. They discovered them with God's help. Every law that man has mastered propelled society to the next level of increase. Let's look at the beginning.

God never begins to end, thus in *Genesis* we read a phrase that makes no sense to the natural. **"Evening and morning…"**

"And God called the light Day, and the darkness he called Night. And the evening and the morning were the first day." Genesis 1:5 KJV

We live and move from beginning to end. Thus morning and evening would be our first day. Zero always precedes the number one… Out of zero one became. Out of nothing everything else became. God will always be the zero that precedes the one.

God created light and everything that light is… which is how light became. Now the power of this truth is that God didn't make the sun until the fourth day, yet light was made on the first day. Out of evening light began. The light that He made was made before the light we now see, feel and use for energy, the sun. God pulls the light out of Him and there was light before there was a sun. **Hebrews 11:3** gives us some clarity on how God did it. We know that the worlds were framed by the Word of God.

"And God said, Let there be light: and there was light. And God saw the light, that it was good: and God divided the light from the darkness." Genesis 1:1, 4 KJV

Out of the "one" God made the many. God made the water and then told the water to create. God made the light and then told the light to divide. God made the earth and then told the earth to create the living creatures. Out of the one came the many.

"And God said, Let the earth bring forth grass, the herb yielding seed, and the fruit tree yielding fruit after his kind, whose seed is in itself, upon the earth: and it was so." And the earth brought forth grass, and herb yielding seed after his kind, and the tree yielding fruit, whose seed was in itself, after his kind: and God saw that it was good." Genesis 1:11-12 KJV

"And God said; Let the waters bring forth abundantly the moving creature that hath life, and fowl that may fly above the earth in the open firmament of heaven. And God created great whales, and every living creature that moveth, which the waters brought forth abundantly, after their kind, and every winged fowl after his kind: and God saw that it was good." Genesis 1:20-21 KJV

"And God said, Let the earth bring forth the living creature after his kind, cattle, and creeping thing, and beast of the earth after his kind: and it was so."
Genesis 1:24 KJV

Everything you will ever need already exists in what God already made. You and I were made out of the earth. We are walking, breathing dirt. God made the earth, and then gave the earth power to create everything else it would ever need. You think, perhaps, that God made us and then put in us the potential to birth everything else we would ever need. Everything you need to become what you've been destined to be is not coming to you but is already in you. You are fearfully and wonderfully made. *(Psalm 139:14)*

"I will praise thee; for I am fearfully and wonderfully made: marvelous are thy works; and that my soul knoweth right well." Psalm 139:14 KJV

We must understand that God can't move in our lives unless we unlock what's already been put in our lives.

This is the reason you have been sought after by the enemy, and this is the reason that the enemy has kept you blind to the revelation of who you are. The revelation of who you are is the power of identity. The difference between a harvest and an inheritance is this, a harvest is the result of something I did... an inheritance is the result of who I am! Wow, this is awesome! Sin is not what you are; sin is the result of something you did. You did it because you haven't recognized yet who you are. Sin is not the problem!

Whatever you need in your life is already in your house. The seed that God has for increase isn't being made or moving to you because it's already in you. When God spoke the earth into existence the trees, flowers and every kind of plant were in the soil of God's spoken word. God only had to tell the earth to produce what the earth already possessed.

There was a widow in the Bible that was about to lose her son to the creditors. Her husband had died and left her with no savings and an incredible amount of debt.

This widow approaches the Man of God, and inquires for His help. She was in desperate need for a Godly answer to her problem. Now, the answer that the Man of God gave her was not the answer she was looking for. The Prophet asks her, "What do you have?" Her answer, "I have nothing!" Imagine what she must have been thinking... Isn't this man listening to me? How insensitive he must have appeared to her. She needed his help; she was in desperate need of someone who could help her out of her crisis. What does this man of God do? He asks the question… "What do you have?" She had nothing but a pot of oil!

"And Elisha said unto her, what should I do for thee? Tell me, what hast thou in the house? And she said, Thine handmaid hath not any thing in the house, save a pot of oil." 2 Kings 4:2 KJV

That's enough! That's all you need. Go and borrow as many empty pots as you can. Not a little or a few, but borrow as many empty pots as you can believe for.

"Then he said, Go, borrow thee vessels abroad of all thy neighbours, even empty vessels; borrow not a few."
2 Kings 4:3 KJV

This seems crazy! She's already in debt. She's already in need, and what are the instructions of the Man of God? Go and borrow empty pots and then shut yourself in with God and start pouring your pot of oil. Elisha knew that if she would believe and use what she already had, she could create everything she would need. What you have in your house is enough to gain whatever else you need…if you give it to God. She was willing to follow the instructions of a Man of God. The instructions you are willing to follow create the future your able to walk in. The difference between seasons is an instruction.

Every instruction from the Lord will seem illogical but not impossible. Everything you need is already in you.

Let me give you some scriptures to meditate on. Don't rush through these. Many times when I'm reading a book, I rush through the quoted bible verses, just to keep reading what the author is writing. Don't skip these. Each verse will build in you something awesome. *"And I will give thee the treasures of darkness, and <u>hidden</u> riches of secret places, that thou mayest know that I, the LORD, which call thee by thy name, am the God of Israel." Isaiah 45:3 KJV*

"For this commandment, which I command thee, this day, it is not <u>hidden</u> from thee, neither is it far off. It is not in heaven, that thou shouldest say, Who shall go up for us to heaven, and bring it unto us, that we may hear it, and do it? Neither is it beyond the sea, that thou shouldest say, who shall go over the sea for us, and bring it unto us, that we may hear it, and do it? But the word is very <u>nigh unto thee, in thy mouth</u>, and in thy heart, that thou mayest do it." Deuteronomy 30:11-14 KJV

"These things have I spoken unto you, that my joy might <u>remain in you</u>, and that your joy might be full." John 15:11 KJV

"Even as the testimony of Christ was confirmed in you, so that you come short in no gift, eagerly waiting for the revelation of our Lord Jesus Christ, who will also

confirm you to the end, that you may be blameless in the day of our Lord Jesus Christ. God is faithful, by whom you were called into the fellowship of His Son, Jesus Christ our Lord." 1 Corinthians 1:6-9 NKJV

"Being confident of this very thing, that He who has begun a good work <u>in you</u> will complete it until the day of Jesus Christ." Philippians 1:6 NKJV

The power to increase and multiply is within you. All you need to tap into this potential is to set in motion the power of principles. The law of cause and effect is the power to make a movement and cause a reaction. Sow and you reap! Cause and effect! Sin is not the cause; it's the effect of something we are sowing. Sin is not what you're doing; it's the effect of what you're not doing.

The law of cause and effect... you cause your effects.

Sin is not the cause; sin is the effect of a greater and more deadly cause. Sin is not our problem... Once we discover the source of sin we can do away with sinning.

DOCUMENT YOUR JOURNEY

CHAPTER FOUR

THE POWER OF THE WEB!

"Likewise you younger people, submit yourselves to your elders. Yes, all of you be submissive to one another, and be clothed with humility, for "God resists the proud, but gives grace to the humble." Therefore humble yourselves under the mighty hand of God, that He may exalt you in due time"
1 Peter 5:5-7 NKJV

Remember that sin is not the cause; sin is the consequence of something greater. If I keep cleaning out the cobwebs in a room but ignore the spider the webs will always return. The same is true with sin... Sin is the web that the spider keeps weaving. How many times have we seen someone fighting some kind of problem? Whether it is sexual, relational or physical, after a while they always return to their problem of sin? There's a man in my church who returns every three to six months to the habit of crack. This man does everything he can not to use crack.

THE POWER OF THE WEB

He reads his bible, prays, comes to church faithfully, works in a ministry, yet he can't seem to conquer the temptation of using. After he uses, he's right back in church. One thing I can say, at least he keeps fighting. We have tried everything for the past four years. We have yelled, we have cried, and we even tried threatening him. Every time we clean the cobwebs out, they keep coming back. Why? **We can't get this person to face the problem**. We can't get this person to kill the spider. So eventually, no matter how much church he attends, no matter how much time he spends in prayer, no matter how long he sits and studies the Word of God, the spider always returns and he ends up running to do crack. It works the same with anger, bitterness, or with any other sin. We must take the time to kill the spider. I know what someone is thinking right now... we serve an almighty God. All we need to do is have faith and believe. Not so! Faith is not the cleaning agent for our actions. Faith is the key that allows God to act on our behalf.

We have all this power over sin! We don't need that much power to rule sin. Sin isn't hard to rule once you understand what the spider is. What's hard to conquer is the spider, not what the spider leaves behind; his web. (Sin)

THE UTMOST IN GOD IS TO BE IN HIS GLORY

I can say this with passion; if we sin we all will have the same **spider** present when we sin. We all have to deal with the same powerful grip of the spider. Want to know what the spider of sin is? **<u>PRIDE!</u>**

Pride is the opposite of humility. Pride may be a small word, but it carries a deadly virus. This virus will cause you to self exhort, and to develop a lifestyle all about you. I deserve, I need, I want… Pride caused Lucifer to lose sight of the power and might of God. Pride caused Him to become self-motivated. Pride convinced Lucifer that he had what it took to exist without having to be obedient to the laws and principles of God. Look where pride got him! He took the elevator straight to hell. If pride has this much power over one of God's best and most perfect creatures… who do we think we are to not face it and kill it through the power of Jesus name? Every sin can be traced to pride. Remember that sin is nothing but disobedience to God.

Let me give some examples. It was pride that caused Jonah to be buried in the belly of a whale. It was pride that cost Esau his birthright. It was Pride that took Samson's vision. It was pride that betrayed King David, and he lost his son Absolam…

HOW TO TAKE THE ELEVATOR UP AND NOT DOWN…

The highest place in the Kingdom of God is to be in God's Glory. To reach the pinnacle of being a Christian is to be in the presence of God's Glory. What the enemy wants more than anything is to have you fall short of the

Glory of God. (***Romans 3:23***) The greatest gift God gave us was that we can be filled with His Glory.

Religion is under the impression that the height of our walk in the Lord is righteousness, but this is simply not true. Paul says that our righteousness is as filthy rags. Then there are those who believe that the highest in the Lord is faith and hope, not so. Faith and hope will both cease. There will come a day when we will not need faith or hope because we will be with the Lord. Some in church have put their focus on the word **HOLINESS!** They have said that if we live holy we will not sin. So they begin to attach their perceptions to what holiness is. Usually they will start their lists of "don'ts."

- Don't drink…
- Don't smoke…
- Don't steal, kill, lie, etc…
- Don't wear makeup or jewelry...
- Don't, Don't, Don't….

These kinds of people will preach such harsh messages about God and hell with the understanding that if we can build a fear of God and His judgment, people won't sin. No one I know can live a life of rules and eventually not break them. Don't come to the Lord to miss hell or to make heaven. Come to the Lord because you understand that there is no better way of life than to know and be known by Jesus. God speaks more in His word about, love, grace and forgiveness than he does about hell and judgment. God is more centered on what you **"can do"** rather than what you "**can't do**."

There is so much more to do in the Bible than there is not to do. If you spend your time doing the "do's" of the Word you won't have time to do the "don'ts."

Religion is mans attempt to explain God...

Religion is mans attempt to worship God man's way.

Holiness is not something we can put on. It's not a dress, or some piece of clothing that when we put it on we are now holy. Holiness is lived out. It is lived out through our life of pain and pleasure. We are not holy we are walking holy!

The highest in God is to be in the fullness of His Glory!

"For all have sinned and fall short of the glory of God."
Romans 3:23 NKJV

"But we all, with unveiled face, beholding as in a mirror the glory of the Lord, are being transformed into the same image from glory to glory, just as by the Spirit of the Lord." 2 Corinthians 3:17-18 NKJV
"For it is the God who commanded light to shine out of darkness, who has shone in our hearts to give the light of the knowledge of the glory of God in the face of Jesus Christ." 2 Corinthians 4:6 NKJV

The more I live for God and in God, the more I give God Glory. The more I give God Glory the more I really worship God. Where there is no worship there can be no Glory. When we are willing to walk with God, and to obey His truths, we begin to walk in the Glory of the Lord and we are changed. We can't be worshipped if we are the one offering up the worship. Pride can't live in His presence. Flesh cannot stand in the Glory! Flesh can stand in church while we are singing and even while we are preaching. Flesh cannot stand when the true presence of God enters. This is why God said to Moses, "No man has ever seen me and lived." They didn't die immediately, but their flesh couldn't live in his presence. God had to hide Moses in the cleft of the rock and cover him with God. Even when Moses saw the after glory of God's presence he aged ten years. His flesh began to melt. Flesh cannot stand and last in God's glory. *"...That no flesh should glory in His presence."*
1 Corinthians 1: 29 NKJV

We understand that the pinnacle in God is his Glory. Now we must understand what the lowest in Man is.

Our religious background has us under the persuasion that the worst thing in our Christian walk is sin. This is simply not true. Just making that statement has probably rubbed against your spiritual grain. Sin is not the worse thing. Sin is the action of something more hideous, more revolting and more dreadful. There is something that is deeper than the act of sin. There is something that will always cause you to miss the high calling in Christ Jesus. You might think that if it's not sin, then this hideous thing must be **UNBELIEF**.

Yes, that's it! The worst thing you can do is have unbelief. Granted unbelief is bad, and it can stop many of God's blessings, it's not the lowest in man. You might be thinking I know, it is doubt, yea, doubt has to be the worst thing. Doubt robs us of moving into the areas that could unlock our potential and find new seasons yet doubt is not the spider. Is it fear, that's it, fear! Even though fear is the opposite of faith, and can paralyze you from ever making powerful steps of faith, fear is not the spider. There is still something worse. Is it being a non-tither? No, the spider is **PRIDE**!

What caused Satan to miss out? Pride! Pride is self-worship and self-glorification. People who always want the credit for accomplishments are robbing God of His Glory. What do you have that God didn't give you? What accomplishments did you experience that you can't give God the credit for? None! The lowest thing in man is pride.

The dictionary definition of pride is: *"an unduly high opinion of oneself; exaggerated self-esteem; conceit b) haughty behavior resulting from this; arrogance."*
©1995 Zane Publishing, Inc.   ©1994, 1991, 1988 Simon & Schuster, Inc.

The spider that needs to be exterminated is **PRIDE**! Pride is the opposite of humility.

FIFTEEN FACTS ABOUT PRIDE:

1. Pride will keep you from admitting your weaknesses.

Until you can recognize your weaknesses you will never discover your purpose.

"And he said unto me, my grace is sufficient for thee: for my strength is made perfect in <u>weakness</u>. Most gladly therefore will I rather glory in my infirmities, that the power of Christ may rest upon me. Therefore I take pleasure in infirmities, in reproaches, in necessities, in persecutions, in distresses for Christ's sake: for when I <u>am weak</u>, then am I strong." 2 Corinthians 12:9, 10 KJV

Our ability to face our weaknesses allows God the power to fill us with His strengths. God is comfortable with our weaknesses as long as we expose them to him. God will replace them with His presence. Pride will keep us from admitting our weaknesses. We need others to help us and watch us when we have to conquer a weak area of our lives. Pride will convince you that you don't need anybody to help you. Pride says I can help myself.

2. Pride will cause you to despise Godly correction.

Our ability to be corrected is proof that we have the willingness to change. Correction is the end result to every mistake. The mistake has yet to be dealt with until there can be correction. Many are missing their harvest

SIN IS NOT YOUR PROBLEM

simply because they refuse to be told when they are wrong, yet we all make mistakes. Failure is inevitable. We all do wrong. However, failure is not final!

God will forgive someone who does wrong. God is in the forgiveness business. God has the power to forgive and forget. He cannot forgive what we are unwilling to reveal. Pride gives a person the false security that even if they're wrong they can act like they are not. God hates this kind of a person. What they do is become religious. What we are willing to expose gives God the authority to hide it. What we hide gives Satan the authority to expose it. As long as there are un-confessed mistakes there will be a closet for the spider of pride to hide in.

> **OBEDIENCE IS THE PROOF THAT YOU HAVE CONQUERED PRIDE!**

3. Pride will keep you from God's presence.

You can't be a true worshipper if there is pride in your heart. Remember, pride will not stand when the Glory of God is falling. Pride is the reason we don't want God to move in our lives.

4. Pride will keep you from being obedient to God's Word.

Obedience is proof that you have conquered pride. It's not that I'm always willing to be obedient, or that I'm always willing to do what's right. However, I am willing to be made willing to do what is expected of me. Pride always tries to interpret God's instruction to accommodate man's pleasures. When King Saul was told by God to utterly destroy the Amalekites, and to not take anything, he disobeyed. Saul decided that he would take the best of the flocks and he would take the best of the people to make them slaves. Saul, in his, heart was being obedient, except he wasn't doing what God told him to do. He was doing what he assumed was what God told him to do. Samuel, the prophet, immediately exposed the pride of Saul when he arrived on the scene. How does King Saul respond, I took these things to sacrifice to the Lord at Gilgal. Then what Saul says gives us a clear picture of his heart. He asks Samuel to esteem him in front of his men. Pride doesn't follow the total instructions of the Lord.

"And Samuel said, Hath the LORD as great delight in burnt offerings and sacrifices, as in obeying the voice of the LORD? Behold, to obey is better than sacrifice, and to hearken than the fat of rams." 1 Samuel 15:22 KJV

5. Pride will cause you to try to make "something happen" instead of letting it happen.

You won't have to make things happen when you walk humble with the Lord. You won't have to sell yourself or pass out business cards everywhere you go. Why? Your concern in life is not how high you excel but how high you can lift up the name of Jesus. We spend so much wasted effort when we try to do things ourselves instead of letting God set us up for promotion. Whatever promotes you will have to sustain you. If self is promoting you then when times get hard, self will have to be the one that holds you up. Self lacks the power and wisdom to help us when we are in trouble. If God is promoting you, then know that God has the power and wisdom to finish what He started in your life.

6. Pride will produce unbelief.

No person has ever sinned who was not first in unbelief. No person ever arrived in unbelief that didn't first exalt themselves in pride... Thus they chose their own glory instead of God's
Every sin is produced by pride. Humility is the only remedy for pride. It all starts in the mind **(Romans 12:2).** If you don't rule your mind it will rule you. Whatever has your focus has you. Sow a thought, reap a habit; sow a habit, reap a lifestyle; sow a lifestyle, reap a destiny.

Everything we do in life should be giving God the Glory.

"Casting down imaginations and every high thing that exalted itself against the knowledge of God, and bringing into captivity every thought to the obedience of Christ; And having in a readiness to revenge all disobedience, when your obedience is fulfilled."
2 Corinthians 10:5-6 KJV

7. Pride will cause you to hide behind the façade that everything is ok.

All of us tend to hide what we've done when we mess up. We then pray and confess to the Lord and feel that that is enough… that we don't need anyone or anything to help us through our problems. Now, that would be sufficient if that were the only time you committed the infraction, but what about those who keep repeating the same mistake over and over again?

I do believe that we need to confess our sins to the Lord every time we sin, but I am also of the persuasion that we are not going to get through some difficult areas without letting someone in to help us. Someone we can trust to hold us accountable to our actions. Most of us are not going to conquer our addictions, fears or failures without the help of a mentor, spiritual father or friend. Pride usually causes us to hide those things that need to be exposed.

8. Pride always goes before destruction.

"Pride goes before destruction, a haughty spirit before a fall." Proverbs 16:18 NIV

9. Pride always brings disgrace.

"When pride comes, then comes disgrace, but with humility comes wisdom." Proverbs 11:2 NIV

10. Pride produces a life of unrest and arguments.

"Pride only breeds quarrels, but wisdom is found in those who take advice." Proverbs 13:10 NIV

The proud never want to take advice. They are always giving it but are never receiving it. Correction is a sure sign that you have conquered the spirit of pride. Have you ever sat down with some one you have caught in the very act of doing wrong, and instead of being humble and receiving the correction and instruction they need, they sit there and try to turn the conversation, blaming everything and everybody around them as the reason they have messed up. Pride doesn't want to admit it is wrong. The first step to fixing your mistake is to confess you made it. We need to stop blaming everything, and everybody, around us and stand up and confess we have made a mistake.

11. Pride causes us not to seek the Lord.

"In his pride the wicked does not seek him; in all his thoughts there is no room for God." Psalm 10:4 NIV

12. Pride speaks falsely against the righteous.
"Let their lying lips be silenced, for with pride and contempt they speak arrogantly against the righteous." Psalm 31:18 NIV

13. Pride will always deceive you!
"The pride of your heart has deceived you..."

Obadiah 3:3 NIV

Pride gives us false hope. It causes us to hope in ourselves and what happens is that we become confident in man and not in God. Any move toward self-sufficiency is a move away from God.

Never put someone in a position that hasn't dealt with their condition. One of the greatest mistakes many churches make is using everybody that says they are available. What they don't realize is that the person may have a talent to do something, playing an instrument or singing a song, but lack the humility to be placed in a position of influence. Their condition will eventually surface, and what started out to be a blessing, will end up being a burden and could easily destroy the church.

Qualify everybody! Place no one in position that has a spirit of pride. They will fight you when you least expect them to.
"Not a novice, lest being lifted up with pride he fall into the condemnation of the devil." 1 Timothy 3:6 KJV

It will be better to not have a service offered in the church than to start one and have to stop it as fast as you started it. Now, I speak this not by mentorship but by my own experience. I have paid dearly when I have allowed someone in a position without qualifying them first.

14. God hates pride!

"These six things doth the LORD hate: yea, seven are an abomination unto him: 17 A proud look, a lying tongue." Proverbs 6:16-17 KJV

15. Pride causes us to take up the act of sin.

"For all that is in the world, the lust of the flesh, and the lust of the eyes, and the pride of life…" 1 John 2:16 KJV

This is the process of your downward spiral to the act of sinning. Lust of the flesh… what you keep wanting you will eventually have. What your flesh keeps seeking will cause you to lust with your eyes. What you keep looking at you will eventually do or become. Focus is the power to movement. When you see it and desire it, you will eventually talk yourself into doing it. Pride will cause you to disregard the instructions of the Lord.

The spider that needs to be killed is pride!

I close this chapter with these scriptures.
"The fear of the LORD is to hate evil: pride, and arrogancy, and the evil way, and the forward mouth, do I hate." Proverbs 8:13 KJV

"When pride cometh, then cometh shame" Proverbs 11:2 KJV

"The wicked in his pride doth persecute the poor: let them be taken in the devices that they have imagined."

Psalm 10:2 KJV

"Let not the foot of pride come against me, and let not the hand of the wicked remove me. There are the workers of iniquity fallen: they are cast down, and shall not be able to rise." Psalm 36:11-12 KJV

"Better it is to be of an humble spirit with the lowly, than to divide the spoil with the proud. He that handles a matter wisely shall find good: and whoso trusted in the LORD, happy is he." Proverbs 16:19-20 KJV

Every sin is caused by pride... the remedy for pride is humility. Humility is defined as: *having or showing a consciousness of one's defects or shortcomings; not proud; not self-assertive; modest*
Low in condition, rank, or position; lowly; unpretentious
1 *to lower in condition, rank, or position; abase*
2 *to lower in pride; make modest or humble in mind*

Where does all this take place, this pride attitude? It lives in the corridors of our mind. If we don't rule our mind it will rule us. What I am focused on is mastering me. The mind is the most powerful influencer. My father told me when I was a teenager, trying to fight those teenage temptations, "Son, an idle mind is the devils workshop." The word is clear... Guard your heart (mind) for out of it are the issues of life.
"Keep thy heart with all diligence; for out of it are the issues of life." Proverbs 4:23 KJV

The meaning to the word "issues" is boundaries. Your mind has the power to set up your spiritual boundaries. Pride isn't just going to go away because you confessed and ask the Lord to come into your heart. You have to make war against your flesh, which is pride in disguise.

Pray this prayer with me today; ask the Lord to help you deal with your pride. We all have to battle the spirit of pride.

Lord, I come to you today in the name of Jesus. Lord, I ask you to forgive me for walking and acting in the spirit of pride. I know that you hate pride, and pride was the reason that Satan was disobedient to your instructions.

Lord, this day I lay the knife of humility at the root of pride, and I cut down the tree of self-worship and exaltation. I want to be your servant Lord.

I confess today that I will walk according to your words and do what is in your heart instead of mine.

*In the name of Jesus, **AMEN!***

CHAPTER FIVE

SATAN'S GREATEST PLATFORM OF ATTACK

"IF YOU GIVE SATAN A FOOTHOLD, HE'LL TURN IT INTO A STRONGHOLD."

A stronghold is an area of the mind where Satan's ideas reign. It is a structure of logic that is based and rooted in a lie. This is where a lie or false understanding has become truth to the person who is living in a stronghold. A person who is under the influence of a stronghold will begin to rewrite in their logic what they believe is the truth. They will even go to war with you over their conception of the truth. Imagine living your whole life only to find out that you have lived a lie your whole life when you get to the end. No matter how much we try to help these kinds of people they will always live under the influence of a stronghold until they are ready to face the truth. They will never be able to stay very long in any church. The more truth that is revealed by the preaching of God's word, the more they will either have to face their lie, or become angry. Then they will start creating this false imaginary idea that the Pastor is preaching about them, and that He or She doesn't like them, or doesn't want to use them. They eventually say that God has told me to move on. Yea right! God has spoken. No, they are being exposed and their stronghold has to be dealt with. The proof of God's presence is change! If you're not changing and growing in your church, or prayer closet, it's because God is not present. You will want to change when God is in the atmosphere.

A stronghold is anything or thought that is alien to the Word of God. A stronghoid gives the enemy a "command post" to which he can have access to work his falsehood. The enemy does this by giving us misinformation. False feelings and perceived thoughts and injuries that cause someone to be injured and in reality no one has done anything.

Strongholds create false imaginations. Look at what imagination means; *the act or power of forming mental images of what is not actually present; the act or power of creating mental images of what has never been actually experienced or of creating new images or ideas by combining previous experiences.* These people have the problem of exaggerating everything.

"(For the weapons of our warfare are not carnal, but mighty through God to the pulling down of strong holds ;) Casting down imaginations and every high thing that

exalted itself against the knowledge of God, and bringing into captivity every thought to the obedience of Christ."
2 Corinthians 10:4-5 KJV

These are weapons for a successful war against the enemy:
1. *Have faith and trust in God.*
2. *Believe that God can and will protect you.*
3. *Study and use the Word of God daily.*
4. *Pick up your prayer life.*
5. *Learn how to praise and worship God correctly.*
6. *Use those around you... open up and understand the power of fellowship in your local church.*
7. *Depend on God's will.*
8. *Make some solid commitments to obeying the Lord no matter what.*
9. *Get involved with a ministry in your local church.*
10. *Endure, and don't quit. Endurance is a qualifier.*
11. *Trust in the Lord with all your heart.*
12. *Don't try to understand everything just walk by faith.*
13. *Learn the power of real love.*
14. *Confess daily your protection in Jesus name.*
15. *Believe you are worthy for God's best.*

I've been saved for some time now and I must confess we seem to be losing a lot of good warriors.

AVOID DEAD THINGS!

Observing most Christians and their spiritual success, I

have often wondered why it is that the Christians that usually fall in their walk are the ones who have been saved for some time. You would think that those who are newly converted would be the ones who would fall, yet this is not what I have noticed. Yes, many come in and quit the walk within a few months, but these are not my focus. These new converts do very little if any damage to the local church or the body of Christ. No one is making them their focus. I believe that these new converts haven't made the connection that causes them to become a spiritual figure in any ones life... thus they are not yet a target of the enemy!

However, the people who have been saved for sometime... they once had a passion and a spirit of joy. Those who started out with a sense of focus, vision and enthusiasm, and now they sit in our local churches with hollow stares, lifeless worship and no passion or commitment to do anything but complain about what's not being done to satisfy them. I call them the **"living dead."**

Many churches are full of these so-called **"living dead."** It reminds me of an old movie I saw in the eighties. This chemical was released on dead people and it would cause them to wake up from a graveyard of death and walk the streets. They had a form of life, but they were not alive. They were the walking dead. Movement doesn't necessarily mean you're alive. These dead people had all the characteristics of life, yet they were dead. These walking dead people roamed the earth looking for the real living brains of others to eat... eating the living person's brain would somehow ease for a moment their pain of being a walking corpse that moved. They remind me of the horror movie "The Living Dead!"

There might be some spiritual truth to this horror movie. Our churches are full of such people who prey on the knowledge of those who are truly alive to eat their ideas, visions and dreams. They are much worse than those who are graveyard dead; at least those in the graves know they are dead. These "pew sitters" come every week, pay their tithes and don't even know that they are walking, breathing dead people. God hasn't been around them or in them for years, and they are so far removed from his presence that they come every week enter our services and leave the same way they came. They are still angry, still bitter, still talking about others... always learning but never coming to the knowledge of truth. Paul warns us about such people.

"But know this that in the last day's perilous times will come: traitors, headstrong, haughty, lovers of pleasure rather than lovers of God, having a form of godliness but denying its power. And from such people turn away! For of this sort are those who creep into households and make captives of gullible women loaded down with sins, led away by various lusts, always learning and never able to come to the knowledge of the truth."
2 Timothy 3:1-7 NKJV

Notice, this is not talking about drug addicts, adulterous, fornicators, etc. This is talking about church people who at one time where loving, passionate Christians who sought God and godly truths, but somewhere in the process of their search they lost their fire. Let me caution you! Don't get so caught up in the destination, that you stop enjoying the journey. Life is made up of moments. On every interstate they place rest areas so that you can stop long enough to let you shake off the weariness of the travel so you can enjoy the journey. They place maps in these areas with a big red sign on the map that says: **"You are here."** This gives you perspective to where you are in accordance to where you need to be. You must stop long enough in your secret place to focus on God and His spiritual road map, because if you don't know where you are, you will never be able to build spiritual perspective to how and where you need to be.

Don't get so caught up in the furnace that you forget about the fire. Many people who find themselves spiritually dead... didn't start out with their focus on being spiritually dead. They had something inward that caused them to lose the fire, but they keep working at polishing the furnace.

FAVOR KEY *"Don't get so caught up on the furnace that you ignore the fire."*

I'm not doing away with process. I'm not against structure. I'm not advocating that we should just throw away structure and have hours of screaming and shouting in church. That's not my intent. Let me address it this way. The anointing is built on structure. You can't have a powerful move without order. God's only obsession is order. I am not promoting structure to the point that we throw out the spiritual or emotional side. We need both.

Godly order will always bring about the joy, the shout and the emotional side of us. How do we really know we are alive except by our feelings? How do we know the stove is hot if we couldn't feel the burn when we touch it? We are made up of emotions and feelings, but we can't always let our emotions dictate our responses. We need structure. We need feelings.

The fire is important! If we spend all of our time maintaining the furnace's appearance we may forget that the fire needs more wood. We lose the fire, and the furnace has no importance. Religion is furnace oriented and not fire oriented (The Living dead). We have no spiritual power without the fire. Why is it that when someone in those types of churches begins to discover the fire they are cast out or tagged as trouble? Because they begin to remind the old religious people that there is no fire in that house. Instead of embracing the ember of someone's excitement, they throw water of criticism on them until those with the flicker of passion become, as the religious are, dead wood! I use to preach in my early days that God wasn't looking for fire fighters, but He was looking for **FIRE LIGHTERS**!

Paul warns Timothy of such things. These people are religious right down to their socks, having a form of godliness, but denying the power of God around them and in them.

Sin is not our problem. Let's discuss an area that has most of us in question. How can men and women of God who have done so much for God, and God's people, fall and not win in the end? I believe that the answer lies in the understanding of the anointing and how it relates to us.

The Holy Spirit anoints us and without that anointing we will not succeed. We must understand that we are not anointed for ourselves but for others. Ministering to others is what causes my anointing to increase... The anointing to work for the Lord has nothing to do with the power to walk with the Lord. Ministers and lay people walk in the same manner; there is no special anointing to walk with God. The anointing that rest on me through my calling is not the same anointing that dwells in me. Just because I experience success in my workings for God doesn't mean that He's in approval of my life style. There's a verse in the bible that has always been left out in most preaching circles.

"Not every one that saith unto me, Lord, Lord, shall enter into the kingdom of heaven; but he that doeth the will of my Father which is in heaven. Many will say to me in that day, Lord, Lord, have we not prophesied in thy

name? and in thy name have cast out devils? and in thy name done many wonderful works? And then will I profess unto them, I never knew you: depart from me, ye that work iniquity." Matthew 7:21-23 KJV

Just because you call Him Lord, doesn't mean that you have made him Lord over you. He must be in control of your life to be Lord. The bible says that the Lord orders the righteous steps. *"The steps of a good man are ordered by the Lord..." Psalm 37:23.* Our mind immediately paints a picture of all of our ways being established by God when we hear this. If we are in trouble we quote *"the steps of the righteous are ordered by the Lord."* There must be something that the Lord is trying to teach me. Actually, what this really means is that our steps are ordered or commanded by the Lord. God has predetermined your ways. You will walk on firm and prosperous ground if you walk according to His commands. You must be willing to obey your marching orders to be a good person. Many have missed their blessing simply because they refuse to move when God has ordered them to. Your obedience to the Lord's commands will have you walking at His pace; you begin to walk in harmony with Him... Enoch walked with God and was not! What happened? He was so in harmony with the Lord that he left the natural and began walking in the spiritual. Paul says we are being changed from glory to glory.

we know we shouldn't, the time of trouble will come upon us. Then we try to manipulate the Bible to make us feel better. We start quoting bible verse to comfort our flesh. We say things like; *"My steps are ordered by the Lord," "... All things work to the good...," "We are more than conquers..."* These sayings are all true but not when they are spoken out of context.

Watch out! Your wants may speak louder than God's voice. I've noticed that what most people thought they wanted wasn't what they wanted after all. Delayed gratification isn't something we speak much about in this 21st century. Waiting is what is needed to stay focused until the proper timing for us to have what we are wanting. The more we train ourselves to wait, the harder it will be for the enemy to seduce us to sin. We will begin to lust for what we are not supposed to have when we have a craving that we are unable to control. One of the biggest reasons we are in trouble is that we can't refrain from giving our flesh what it wants. Teach your flesh to wait. Don't do anything until the Spirit of God has released it to you. God will always provide where He guides.

Not everyone who says, "Lord, Lord" will enter into heaven but they that do the "will" of my Father. All these people had great success, yet in the end were cast away. The next verse tears me up. When the people begin to pull out their resumes and inform God how much they've done for Him. They said:

"Lord didn't we cast out demons, didn't we do great wonders for you in your name. Yes, but I do not know you. Just because you were anointed to work for me doesn't mean we were in relationship." There has to be a place where you and God spend time together to build a relationship. So the anointing to work for God is different than the anointing to walk with God. Now, I know what you're thinking. How can a loving God use such people and then throw them away? Well, He didn't use them as much as these kinds of Christians have used God. This kind of minister is usually compensated by the way of increase of worldly riches. They use the ministry to build their worldly kingdom. They have increased in wealth and fame. They got caught up in the furnace instead of keeping their walk close to the fire of the Lord. They have been well paid. Sad isn't it, to live your whole life doing something and lose your soul in the end. Don't make this mistake. Make everything you do about Jesus. Do everything with Him in your focus. Jesus, nothing more and nothing less…

THE QUESTION IS NOT DO YOU KNOW HIM, BUT DOES HE KNOW YOU?

Finishing our life and being able to walk in God's presence is more important than what we did or what we are doing. Maybe we should spend sometime studying and learning not how we can know God, but how God can know us. The power of finishing is greater than the power of prosperity in the world. Just because we know someone doesn't mean they have any idea who we are. The ability to receive and be apart of someone is that they know you. This is what I perceive the Lord is saying to us.

Read these verses and let them sink in:

"Teach me to do thy will; for thou art my God: thy spirit is good; lead me into the land of uprightness. Quicken me, O LORD, for thy name's sake: for thy righteousness' sake bring my soul out of trouble."
Psalm 143:10-11 KJV

"Whatsoever thy hand findeth to do, do it with thy might; for there is no work, nor device, nor knowledge, nor wisdom, in the grave, whither thou goes."
Ecclesiastes 9:10 KJV

"For it is God which worketh in you both to will and to do of his good pleasure. Do all things without murmurings and disputings." *Philippians 2:13-14 KJV*

"Make you perfect in every good work to do his will, working in you that which is well pleasing in his sight, rough Jesus Christ; to whom be glory for ever and ever. Amen." *Hebrews 13:21 KJV*

Let me give you a powerful revelation… here's a pattern to walk by
- Abel worshipped God.
- Enoch walked with God.
- Noah worked for God.
- Abraham waited on God and Moses saw God.

Worship builds the proper foundation, so that the power of worship can produce the ability to walk with God. If you walk properly with the Lord you will begin to understand His heart and burden. The call will fall on your shoulders because the Holy Spirit is filling your heart. Your work will be full when your heart is full. You'll burn for God, but you wont burn out! Working brings about a faith level that has you always waiting for God to pull you to the next season. Faith is the power to wait on God, and when you worship while you wait you will see God!

It's possible to be so focused on the work that you forget how to walk with God. This is very dangerous because you will assume that because you're being successful in your work God is in approval of your lifestyle. The sad truth is you'll have a great ministry, and do great things, but when it comes to the end you will hear God say. *"But I don't know you. Now leave my presence."* The truth is, God isn't as productive motivated as we are. He tends to be more relational oriented than productive oriented. That's not to say that God doesn't expect us to produce, but He doesn't want you to trade off your walk for your work. God expects us to produce. He commanded us to multiply. God expects us to walk with a spirit of excellence; He just doesn't want you to produce your success without staying focused on Him. Any attempt to succeed without God's help is going to cost you in the end.

I've been to big ministries, and when I walked into their buildings and saw how much they have accomplished, I would just sit there and feel at awe at all the splendor of what I was looking at. My first thought would be, "This Man of God must pray and have a walk with God that no one could compare to. They must walk in such power and love." Then I would evaluate my ministry and begin to feel squashed and question my own calling, "What's wrong with me Lord? Why haven't I advanced to this kind of level?" The truth is that what we see isn't necessarily the result of how they are living. It's better to enter heaven with a small ministry doing small things, and in the process you kept your relationship with God, than to enter the presence of God and all you can boast about is the buildings and the status of your accomplishments. When you look up and see God you realize I don't know this God. To hear the Lord say, *"I don't know you!"* You're a child of iniquity.

Dr. Mike Murdock of the Wisdom Center says, "Any move to self sufficiency is a move away from God."
Don't get caught up in worshipping the furnace and forget the fire that is contained within.

Labor to know God's voice… Labor to be a God pleaser and not a man pleaser… Who you are matters to God as much as what you're doing.

Learn to focus on your walk as much as your work! Don't let the blessings of God take you where your character can't keep you.

CHAPTER SIX

THE POWER TO WIN IS WITHIN!

*"For He whom God has sent speaks the words of God,
for God does not give the Spirit by measure..."*
John 3:34

First, we must understand what eternity is... If you believe that eternity is some far off place in time and space where we are heading, or a place called heaven or hell, you have already missed the mark. It is this mentality that pushes us off the reality of our actions to a distant place. We are then relieved from our present actions. We have been conditioned to make the word "eternal" a meaning that only exists with God, Satan, Angels and Demons. These are the eternal beings. The power of this mentality is that we miss the true power of eternity.

We must understand that we are also eternal beings and for us, eternity is NOW! Joy is the reward for discerning the divine deposit in the moment when we learn that we can only live in the moment. Life isn't what we can do tomorrow; life is what we are doing right now. I've heard someone say don't put off tomorrow what you could do today. Then truth is you will never live in your tomorrow you will only live in your today. When tomorrow comes you will wake up and rename it today.

If you can't plan your moments then you can't plan your day. If you can't plan your day then you will never be able to plan your life. It is true with control that if you can't control your actions in the moment, you won't be able to control your actions for the day. If you can't control your actions for the day then you won't be able to control your actions in your future… What you are doing daily is deciding what you are becoming permanently. The power of your destiny lives within the power of your mind.

You can't discover what God has assigned for you until you are willing to let God in your moment. You can live a sin free life if you want to. Just live it moment by moment. I once had to counsel a teenager who was crying about always giving into temptation. My comment to him was, "Can you live for God and not do wrong for one hour?" His answer, "Well, yes I can." My response to him was to quit stressing out over what you might do Friday night, and just live for God one hour at a time. Every hour you live a sin free hour, gives you the victory to live a sin free day. The more success you have under your feet the more victory you walk in. This success causes you to want to continue to walk in victory more than walking in sin. Once you have conquered the day-by-day routine you will discover that hours turn into

days, and days turn into months and months turn into years. You have now lived a life with out falling into sin and you did it hour by hour.
"Do not boast about tomorrow, for you do not know what a day may bring forth." Proverbs 27:1 NIV

"Therefore do not worry about tomorrow, for tomorrow will worry about itself. Each day has enough trouble of its own." Matthew 6:34 NIV

Living a Christian life isn't hard, if you live it moment by moment. Learn to extract the goodness of God in the moment. Just because you haven't received your major harvest for your seeds yet, there is still increase coming to you in every moment. Eternity is now! You are not going to die; you are going to live forever. The only thing that is going to die is your body. Your flesh is going to die, but what you are is not flesh. You are a spirit being that is housed in the body of flesh. The spirit will still be alive when the body dies. Your eternity is now! What you are doing now will be what you'll have to face forever. What you do in the moment has eternal consequences good or bad. Learn how to make every moment count for the good. I don't want to leave you here with fear about mistakes and failures in the moment. The power of grace gives us the freedom to face our mistakes and confess them to Jesus. His grace has the power to forgive us and forget our momentary plunders and gives us a new day, every day.

The Word of God says that the mercies of God are new every morning. God made us to be new every morning. Every 365 days there's a new year. Every 30 days there's a new month. Every 24 hours there's a new day and every 60 minutes there's a new hour. God is into making things new. Learn to confess to God your weakness and let His strengths become who you are. Live in the moment! Stop wasting your life. When your children do something, stop and notice them in the moment. When your wife has spent the day cleaning up the house or preparing a special meal walk in and notice the moment. When you see someone doing something for you be sure to recognize the moment. You will become stress free when you understand the only real power you have is to rule your moments.

When you ask the Holy Spirit to come in, He doesn't come in by measure He comes in fully. When He entered, all of the fullness of the Godhead entered with Him (Holy Spirit). You are not being filled with God's measure; you have been filled with God's fullness. Remember *John 3:34*, God did not give the spirit by measure. He gave the Holy Spirit fully. Everything you need isn't coming down from heaven; it's coming out of you.

How do we unlock the fullness of what God has stored up in us? In a single word the answer is; understanding. The more wisdom you gain and the more understanding you walk in unlocks in measure what has been stored in full.

The Word declares *"Wisdom is the principle thing, above all else get understanding"* **Proverbs 4:7.** The more we grow in our knowledge of God's principles the more increase and power we will walk in. Just because all of God is in us doesn't' mean we have the wisdom and knowledge to use that kind of power.

"When I was a child, I spake as a child, I understood as a child, I thought as a child: but when I became a man, I put away childish things. For now we see through a glass, darkly; but then face-to-face: now I know in part; but then shall I know even as also I am known. And now abideth faith, hope, charity, these three; but the greatest of these is charity." 1 Corinthians 13:11-13 KJV

When I was a child a spoke as a child; I thought as a child; I made childish decisions. When I was a child I understood as a child. There comes a time when I stop being a child and I start being an adult. My responsibilities change when I make the adult transition. My goals change. My desires change. A child sees in part. A child's only goal is what he or she can have immediately to satisfy their wants. Adults have learned that we can't have everything we want when we want it. We understand that we must work and pay our bills if we want to maintain a standard of living. We come to the knowledge that things have a price. They cost us time and energy.

Look at this passage next:

"Now I say, that the heir, as long as he is a child, different nothing from a servant, though he be lord of all; But is under tutors and governors until the time appointed of the father. Even so we, when we were children, were in bondage under the elements of the world: But when the fullness of the time was come, God sent forth his Son, made of a woman, made under the law, To redeem them that were under the law, that we might receive the adoption of sons. And because ye are sons, God hath sent forth the Spirit of his Son into your hearts, crying, Abba, Father. Wherefore thou art no more a servant, but a son; and if a son, then an heir of God through Christ. Howbeit then, when ye knew not God, ye did service unto them which by nature are no gods. But now, after that ye have known God, or rather are known of God, how turn ye again to the weak and beggarly elements, whereunto ye desire again to be in bondage?" Galatians 4:1-9 KJV

You can have all the money in the world tied to you by your connection to your father. However, until you come to maturity you are not going to have access to those funds. This passage is clearly letting us know that everything we need, we already have. Everything has already been stored up for us and is ours. We just can't have access to it, because we are still children. Our focus as a child is all about us. Give me, satisfy me, and take care of me... The older my son gets, the more time I seem to spend having conversations with him. I now tend to give him more money. When he needed a ten-dollar bill and all I had was a twenty, I would go to the store and get the exact change. Why? When he was younger he lacked the understanding of what the value of money was. Now I'll hand him the twenty and tell him to bring me back the change. What does he do? He is obedient to bring me back the change. This has now given me the power as his father to release more than he needs. Why? I can now trust him with what's mine. The same works with God. The more God can trust us, the more He will release the fullness of what we are living out by measure. This is a powerful principle!

All of heaven is in us. The fullness of the Godhead is in us. WOW! Let's look at another verse:

"From whom his whole family in heaven and on earth derives its name. I pray that out of his glorious riches he may strengthen you with power through his Spirit in your inner being, so that Christ may dwell in your hearts through faith. And I pray that you, being rooted and established in love, may have power, together with all the saints, to grasp how wide and long and high and deep is the love of Christ, and to know this love that surpasses knowledge-that you may be filled to the measure of all the fullness of God. Now to him who is able to do immeasurably more than all we ask or imagine, according to his power that is at work within us, to him be glory in the church and in Christ Jesus throughout all generations, for ever and ever! Amen."
Ephesians 3:15-21 NIV

Notice... *"Strengthen you with power through his spirit in your inner being. So that Christ may dwell in your hearts through faith..."*

How does this power work? In **verse 18** the word **"grasp"** means understanding. This is so you may understand how deep, wide, long, and high is the love of Christ, and that we may be filled to the measure of **all the fullness of God.** Notice "to be able to do"... is at work, where? <u>In us!</u> Where is the ability to do exceedingly, abundantly above all exist? <u>In us!</u>

We keep sitting around the house or in our churches waiting and praying for God to do something. Maybe we should consider what the Word so clearly reveals. That God has already done it. God is now waiting on us to unlock our understanding. The more we unlock our wisdom the more we are going to do what Jesus did.

Let me put some balance here. Wisdom without revelation is divisive. The word says in revelation that there is a bottomless pit. Jesus is the foundation of all we do. If we don't build this increase and power on the foundation of Jesus we will be cast into the bottomless pit. Wisdom without revelation and revelation that isn't based on the foundation, Jesus, means your life will be bottomless.
Everything you're going to become, and are destined to become, isn't off in the distance of your future. It is not

coming down from heaven, nor does it have to be prayed for or believed for. It's not locked up in some book, or in some college degree. Everything you are becoming and are destined to become can be found in one place, **YOU!** God did not give the Spirit by measure; He gave the Spirit to us in full. You are not being filled, you are filled! Let me build understanding here. I do believe in the second work of grace. You must confess and ask for the gift of the spirit. We call this the "baptism of the Holy Spirit." I don't believe that the Holy Spirit is falling on you. I believe He's released from you. The Word says that out of our bellies will flow rivers of living water.

- Where is this living water?
- Where is this power to perform miracles?
- Where does the power of greatness live? In you!

WHEN ARE WE FILLED?
The Old Testament work of the Spirit was to perform acts for God. The Holy Spirit was not able to live within those He had to use. The Holy Spirit would come upon those that were chosen to be used and perform the miracle acts that God had placed for those to be used. When the miracle was over the Holy Spirit would have to leave.

The Holy Spirit was only around for the specific moment because of the sinful state of man's nature, and because man in the Old Testament was not yet forgiven and cleansed from the guilt and stain for man's sinful nature.

"Even the Spirit of truth; whom the world cannot receive, because it seeth him not, neither knoweth him: but ye know him; for he dwelleth with you, and shall be in you. I will not leave you comfortless: I will come to you. Yet a little while, and the world seeth me no more; but ye see me: because I live, ye shall live also. At that day ye shall know that I am in my Father, and ye in me, and I in you." John 14:17-20 KJV

There was a time we could not receive the spirit because we did not see him nor did we know him. Why? He was not able to live in us. Notice these two words in this passage:

1. "…For he dwells with you."
2. "Shall be in you…"

I love the last part of *John 14:20* Jesus said... ***"At that day you shall know that I am in my Father, and you in me, and I in you."*** How is Jesus in us? When does the Holy Spirit fill us? The Spirit fills us only when He comes in us.

"If ye abide in me, and my words abide in you, ye shall ask what ye will, and it shall be done unto you. Herein is my Father glorified, that ye bear much fruit; so shall ye be my disciples." John 15:7-8 KJV

"These things have I spoken unto you, that my joy might remain in you, and that your joy might be full John 15:11KJV

"That my joy might remain in you, and that your joy might be full." How do you walk in peace and joy? If you abide in God, and His words abide in you, you will ask what you will and it will be done unto you! Do you want to glorify God? Then produce much. Walk now according to the Word of God. Do you want Jesus to abide in you? You must abide in His Word. The Greek word for abide, *"meno"* means: *"to stay in a given place, state, relation, or expectancy."* If you stay in a given place, state, relation, or expectancy with God then you will ask what you will and it will be done unto you. Herein will my father be glorified, that you bear much fruit. God is glorified when we continually increase.

Joy doesn't come from any one thing, or any one person. The fruit of joy is peace. Joy is the resource that is within you. When you abide in the Word and The Word is abiding IN YOU, you will ask what you will and God, which is in heaven, will do it. This you will do so that God's joy might remain in you.

What is joy? The dictionary states that joy is: *a very glad feeling; happiness; great pleasure or delight.* Jesus says that in you, through the Holy Spirit, is the feeling of gladness, the power of happiness, the resource of great pleasure and delight. Joy is the peace of God around you, because the power of God is released from within you. When Jesus' joy remains in you, your joy remains full. Stop living a life of empty dreams and hollow visions. Put Jesus where He belongs, and you will experience joy that the world cannot offer.

After God created the earth, everything that God made came out of the earth. Everything we see around us, including us, came from the one thing God made; the earth. God placed enough resources in the earth, to produce everything the earth needed to survive. WOW! This is amazing. God made the water and told the water to produce. God made man, and spoke over man and said produce. Everything we need now and for our destiny isn't going to fall from heaven, nor is it somewhere off in the future. The power to increase and produce is within us. Man has the potential to create with his faith everything he will ever need to fulfill his purpose, and we have a problem believing in God. The reason men fail is not that they lack potential or ability...no sir! Men fail because they lack the ability to understand the law of timing *(Ecclesiastes 3)*. We just established the power that is residing within man. You can be the most gifted man, have all knowledge, and understand all things; however, if you don't know what time it is, you will step out to soon and fail. Your failure will have nothing to do with potential, but have everything to do with timing. Entering a season before you're supposed to be there can be devastating. Learn to understand not only your power and potential, but also when to step, and when to stand.

Stop praying prayers that have no meaning. Stop asking God for stuff that already exists in you. You are fearfully and wonderfully made. Mankind has a purpose. You have a purpose. Take the time necessary to discover that purpose God has already placed in you. Discoveries will always decide your season.

You must labor to understand every moment and to hear God's voice. The sheep know his voice and another they will not follow. Here's something nice I read on the Internet the other day about a moment. I don't know who said it first, but I like what I read.

- *"Happy moments, praise God"*
- *"Difficult moments, seek God"*
- *"Quiet moments, worship God"*
- *"Painful moments, trust God"*
- *"In every moment, thank God"*

Learn to extract the joy that is deposited into every moment, and remember that the power to win comes from within!

Below are some more scriptures for you to read and study.
"For it is not ye that speak, but the Spirit of your Father which speaketh in you."Matthew 10:20 .KJV

"But ye are not in the flesh, but in the Spirit, if so be that the Spirit of God dwell in you. Now if any men have not the Spirit of Christ, he is none of his. And if Christ be in you, the body is dead because of sin; but the Spirit is life because of righteousness. But if the Spirit of him that raised up Jesus from the dead dwell in you, he that raised up Christ from the dead shall also quicken your mortal

bodies by his Spirit that dwelleth in you."
Romans 8:9-11 KJV

"Being confident of this very thing, that he which hath begun a good <u>work in you</u> will perform it until the day of Jesus Christ."Philippians 1:6 KJV

"For it is God which works <u>in you</u> both to will and to do of his good pleasure. Do all things without murmurings and disputing."Philippians 2:13-14 KJV

"Make you perfect in every good work to do his will, <u>working in you</u> that which is well pleasing in his sight, through Jesus Christ; to whom be glory for ever and ever. Amen."Hebrews 13:21 KJV

"...because ye are strong, and the word of God <u>abideth in you</u>, and ye have overcome the wicked one."
1 John 2:14 KJV

"But the anointing which ye have received of him <u>abideth in you</u>." 1 John 2:27 KJV

"Ye are of God, little children, and have overcome them: because greater is he that <u>is in you</u>, than he that is in the world."1 John 4:4 KJV

CHAPTER SEVEN

FIVE ENEMIES THAT MUST BE DESTROYED!

"Moses my servant is dead; now therefore arise, go over this Jordan, thou, and this entire people, unto the land, which I do give to them, even to the children of Israel."
Joshua 1:2 KJV

The second half of the spiritual journey for the people of God has begun. Joshua, who has been the second in command for so many years, is now being forced to the forefront, a position he's been waiting on for almost forty years. The first thing we discover is that God must let Joshua understand that Moses is dead. It's obvious that Joshua was a great assistant. One must first be a good follower before he can be a leader. Joshua had proven time and time again that he was a good follower. He stays committed and loyal throughout Moses' reign. A person who keeps trying to get promoted never succeeds properly. If he or she is self promoted, then that's what will have to sustain them in crisis. Whatever promotes you has to be able to hold you in trouble times. This is why it is imperative that we learn how to wait on God for our promotion. If God is the one who is bringing the increase, then it will be God who is obligated to sustain you when hell or trouble is trying to demote you. This is the very reason that David doesn't take Saul's life when God kept handing King Saul over to David. It was a test. Was David going to wait on the timing of God, or was he going to promote himself. How about you? Are you going to wait on the Lord, or are you going to make it happen yourself?

> **WHAT PROMOTES YOU MUST BE ABLE TO SUSTAIN YOU**

LET IT HAPPEN, DON'T MAKE IT HAPPEN!

Do what it takes to improve your self… Read, study, take classes and find a mentor. Give God something to promote but in the end wait on the Lord.

Joshua never rallied to be promoted. He never questioned his leader's decisions, even though Moses didn't always make the proper choices. The assistant always has to be willing to pay the same price as the leader without being able to increase as the leader increases. Every time we see Moses seeking God on the mountain of God, we see Joshua always present. Joshua was never allowed to make the climbs as high as Moses, but nonetheless he had to go and endure the same elements and the same sacrifices that his mentor had to endure. Joshua was never allowed to be in the place to see or hear the voice of God. Joshua loved Moses and was loyal to his spiritual father. God raised Joshua to finish what Moses started.

We must understand that there is always someone more anointed than the leader. A good mentor knows that they need to be willing to pull those, who are destined for the next season, around them and mentor them. Moses was anointed to bring out the people of God, but he lacked the ability to change and adjust his theology into being anointed to take them in. There are those who have the ability to get people out of their mess but lack the potential to bring them into their destiny and calling. Now, the problem with not being anointed to do both is that when we bring someone out of their mess, and are unable to plug them into their future, they become stagnate and bored. They will eventually go back to where they came from. We must be able as leaders to do both or have a system set up to take care of our weaknesses.

Joshua knew how to serve before he became the man to lead. The same was true for Elisha, who served Elijah for fifteen years. These men possess a quality that allowed them to be promoted by God with such power and authority. They were able to do more, and succeed quicker, than their mentors. What took Moses and Elijah a lifetime to do, Joshua and Elisha did in a day.

God had to encourage Joshua and inform him to let the old die for the new things to transpire.

Favor Key: "The enemy to a present move of God is the last move of God."

You must be willing to let go of your past to move into your future. Joshua is now to become the spiritual leader of God's people, and the first thing that God wants Joshua to know is that Moses is dead. Let go of what was, and build what is to become... *The same is true for us*. We all have a past. We all have things in our past that try to creep up in our minds to destroy everything we are trying to do in our present that will determine our future. This is why God's Word tells us: ***"...but this one thing I do, forgetting those things which are behind, and reaching forth unto those things which are before..." Philippians 3:13***

Joshua has some big shoes to fill. He must begin to know who he is, and that he has been trained by the best, but he's not Moses, he's Joshua. God didn't want Joshua to be Moses; He wanted Joshua to be who He had ordained him to be! Again, the same is true for us. It's easy to try to be someone else with so many good spiritual leaders around us. God can't anoint those who are trying to be someone they are not. God will anoint those who will just be themselves. God let Joshua know what was, is not what is! Then God gives Joshua a word of encouragement and instruction.
"Every place that the sole of your foot shall tread upon, that have I given unto you, as I said unto Moses."
Joshua 1:3 KJV

SIN IS NOT YOUR PROBLEM

"Only be thou strong and very courageous, that thou mayest observe to do according to all the law, which Moses my servant commanded thee: turn not from it to the right hand or to the left, that thou mayest prosper whithersoever thou goest." Joshua 1:7 KJV

God let Joshua know that as He was with Moses so would He be with him. He also made it clear that Joshua must adhere to the same obedience to God's Word as Moses did. Joshua doesn't have to be Moses, but he does have to follow the same principles that Moses followed. We have the same power for us. We are not to be what others are, but we are to operate in the same principles that others did to succeed.

This is vital. We must understand that God isn't looking to make carbon copies of those who have led us in times past or who are leading us today. However, He does expect us to adhere to the same principles. Jesus had to submit to them, and so did every other Godly leader who accomplished anything. Our methods should change with time, but our message should always be the same. Our method is not what is causing us to malfunction, but our motives could be what are killing us.

Joshua isn't some young man taking over. He's now in his eighties. He's been through slavery, forty years in the wilderness and now he has to take over, goes to war and has to fight to claim his promise. God takes no time in training this leader. First, they have a massive victory at

Jericho and experience a supernatural hand of favor. Then, they move to their next quest, mind you, a smaller and much easier city to conquer than Jericho. It was the city of Ai. Joshua experienced the thrill of victory then the pain of defeat. Joshua learns fast that it doesn't pay to do things your own way. It's better to enquire of the Lord over every situation, and enter no battle with the assumption *"just because they are small we can win."*

We have a hidden message on how to conquer the power of sin in Joshua chapter 9. Joshua teaches us a valuable lesson on how to do this.

Joshua made a treaty with the people called the Gibeonites.

"And Joshua made peace with them, and made a league with them, to let them live: and the princes of the congregation sware unto them." Joshua 9:15 KJV

Five kingdoms bind together and rise up to fight the Gibeonites and destroy them for making a treaty with Joshua and the children of God.

"Wherefore Adoni-zedek king of Jerusalem sent unto Hoham king of Hebron, and unto Piram king of Jarmuth, and unto Japhia king of Lachish, and unto Debir king of Eglon, saying..." Joshua 10:3 KJV

Joshua was called on by his new covenant servants that

needed help. So, Joshua immediately gathers his army and heads for war on behalf of the Gibeonites. When Joshua prevailed, and when these kings saw that the army of God was winning, they fled.

"But these five kings fled, and hid themselves in a cave at Makkedah." Joshua 10:16 KJV

This is what the spirit of control does. It will raise its ugly head to defeat anyone who has made a connection to the right people. The right connection will always draw out those who will try to destroy you. King Adoni-zedek possessed a spirit of control and set out to destroy those who connected to Joshua.

The right connection will help and protect you from those who are trying to destroy you. The wrong connection will always destroy you.

How to identify the right connection by asking:
1. Do they defend you in your absence?
2. Are your enemies their enemies?
3. Do they rejoice over your rewards and successes?
4. Do they cover your weaknesses?

If so, then you have made a good connection.

Joshua shows up, and God holds the sun still and stops time for Joshua to fulfill his mission. Then, God spoke to Joshua to go after these five kings, to destroy them and make no treaty with them.

" And it came to pass, when they brought out those kings unto Joshua, that Joshua called for all the men of Israel, and said unto the captains of the men of war which went with him, Come near, put your feet upon the necks of these kings. And they came near, and put their feet upon the necks of them." Joshua 10:24 KJV

"And afterward Joshua smote them, and slew them, and hanged them on five trees: and they were hanging upon the trees until the evening." Joshua 10:26 KJV

Joshua is instructed to hang the kings, take no prisoners and to destroy all wickedness. Sin has been running wild long enough.

The names of these kings have significant meanings. I believe that God was giving us a secret look at what we need to do with these five spirits.

First, there was ***Adoni-zedek, king of Jerusalem,*** which means *pride and self-righteousness.*
Pride always leads to self-righteousness. Now, I'm not going to spend a lot of time on pride, because I've already covered this subject in a previous chapter. Pride is ugly and will always lead to destruction.

The dictionary defines self-righteousness as: *"filled with or showing a conviction of being morally superior, or more righteous than others; smugly virtuous"*
©1995 Zane Publishing, Inc.   ©1994, 1991, 1988 Simon & Schuster, Inc.

Place your foot on this demons neck and choke him out of your life.

Second, there was ***Hoham, king of Hebron.*** Hoham represents the spirit of laziness. The spirit of hesitation… Hesitation can be very costly. When God speaks an instruction to you, He takes hesitation as disobedience. Stop hesitating. Stop being lazy about certain things! Welfare in this country is proof that there is a demon of laziness is in control. There is a problem when women are getting up and going to work while a healthy man sits on the couch-waving goodbye to her. This country is filled with so many deadbeat dads and husbands it is sickening. Come on! Let's get with the program! If you're reading this book and you are healthy then get off your lazy rear end and get a job! Not only have we seen a spirit of laziness in our homes, what about the church? No one seems to be interested in God's house. Why is it that we have 300 people on Sundays and only 140 people on Wednesday? No one has the time for church or Godly things anymore. Of course, you're going to feel tired after a day of work…but get up and spend some time with your wife… with your children. Do something besides sit there and wait for the next day. We are surrounded with lazy givers, lazy workers and lazy tithers. I bind the spirit of laziness in the church. I rebuke this demon of control that is causing people to always feel tired and fatigued. Remember, when fatigue comes in, faith goes out.

"The way of the slothful man is as a hedge of thorns."
Proverbs 15:19 KJV

"One who is slack in his work is brother to one who destroys." Proverbs 18:9 NIV

"The sluggard's craving will be the death of him, because his hands refuse to work." Proverbs 21:25 NIV

"As the door turneth upon his hinges, so doth the slothful upon his bed." Proverbs 26:14 KJV

The third king was **Piram, king of Jarmuth;** He represents a spirit of no self-control. The bible calls this a spirit of lawlessness, or lasciviousness. Now, I know what you're doing right now... your thinking what in the world does lasciviousness mean?

Webster defines lascivious as:
"...Characterized by or expressing lust or lewdness; wanton; tending to excite lustful desires"

It's another word for lust! God wants us to stop this spirit of doing whatever we want to do. Just do what feels good mentality. This spirit is what's causing rape, child molestation, homosexuality, teen pregnancy and child pornography. Just to name a few.

We need to bind together and stop this demon that has destroyed our churches and families all over this country.

SIN IS NOT YOUR PROBLEM

Divorce is at an all time high. Men and women can't control their desires and are leaving one another to chase what they think is better. You know, *"the grass is greener mentality."* The grass isn't greener; in fact when you get there you find out it wasn't grass at all... Satan just painted asphalt to look like grass.

"For from within, out of the heart of men, proceed evil thoughts, adulteries, fornications, murders, Thefts, covetousness, wickedness, deceit, lasciviousness, an evil eye, blasphemy, pride, foolishness: All these evil things come from within, and defile the man."
Mark 7:21-23 KJV

"Now the works of the flesh are manifest, which are these; Adultery, fornication, uncleanness, lasciviousness..." Galatians 5:19 KJV

"Who being past feeling have given themselves over unto lasciviousness, to work all uncleanness with greediness."
Ephesians 4:19 KJV

The fourth king was **Japhia, king of Lachish;** He represents *self-elevation.* This person is always promoting their agenda. They are never looking out for others, but they are always looking out for what they can get out of people. They are leeches... parasites...

A leech is a person who clings to another to gain some personal advantage to drain them dry.

"The leech has two daughters. 'Give! Give!' they cry."
Proverbs 30:15 NIV

I was preaching to a group of preachers the other day. God spoke to me and told me to speak over these preachers a word of encouragement and confirmation. I told them that God said not to be shook up about those who are leaving their life. God is removing what doesn't belong, so that He can put in place around them what does belong. He is removing those who are not for you.

Favor key *"Just because people say they are for us, doesn't mean they are. Not everyone who says they are your enemy is trying to destroy you."*

When you see an exodus taking place it's because those who are leaving didn't qualify for your harvest. If those around you can't believe in you, then they are no good for you. If someone around you can't discern your worth and value, they disqualify for a relationship with you. Cut off these leeches. All they want to do is deplete you of your energy and resources. They will unplug from you when you are dried up, dead and there is no more of you to give. They will unplug from your ministry and find someone, or some other ministry, to suck dry.

Let me go further; aren't you tired of people who come in your churches, or businesses, and tell you their resume'? They can't just come in, sit with you and carry on a normal conversation without telling you all about themselves and their accomplishments. I run from such people. I can't stand to be around someone who always has to talk about themselves. They are parasites.

The fifth and last king was **Debir, king of Eglon;** this king represents the *critical and judgmental* spirit. Those who can never enter your atmosphere without criticizing and judging everything you do.

This is a murdering spirit of words and attitude. Those who are allowed to stay around your church or friends with this spirit will begin to build an atmosphere of questioning every decision you make. They will talk to those that are around them criticizing and judging everything you do, until those that use to believe in you will start questioning your ability as their leader. Cut these kinds of people off quick.

I had this man in my church that had a good amount of money, and he would pay off certain bills in the church. He even got behind my books and helped me pay off the cost of printing. I kept him around for some time, but it cost me more in the end. He was one of those who always thought they were smarter and better than those who were trying to lead him and teach him. He never would stop and listen to you. Every conversation was a burden. No matter what you said he would always want to debate you. He was too smart for his own good.

Every decision was criticized and scrutinized until you would just want to take out a knife and cut off his tongue. I would always run to the furthest side of the table from him when we would sit down around the table with others. Others would be so mad at me for placing them around him. There complaint was he never shuts up. You know what, everybody I know that knows him to this day still says the same thing about him.

I've been in ministry for twenty-four years. I've preached and studied God's Word. I have a Masters Degree in counseling and a Doctorate in Divinity. Every time I did something he would comment and tell me all the mistakes that I did. Now, let me ask you something. Do you want to hang out with someone who has a critical spirit?

Criticism is the death gargle of a non-achiever. The bible says judge not lest you be judged. I would hate to be this guy on judgment day... wouldn't you? Qualify those whom you let in your atmosphere. It's easier to keep them out than it is to get them out. God told Joshua to kill them, destroy them and make no treaty with them. The same rings true for us today. We are going to have to deal with these five demons of control if we want to continue a sin free life. Stick your spiritual foot on their neck and push until their neck snaps in two. In the name of the Lord Jesus, I speak a *Psalm 91* wall of protection around you. I come into agreement with you over these five spirits.

SIN IS NOT YOUR PROBLEM

(Adoni-zedek, pride and self-righteousness; Hoham, laziness and slothfulness; Piram, no self-control, lasciviousness; Japhia, self-elevation, self-promotion; and Debir, a critical and judgmental spirit)

I pray that God is going to give you the power to utterly destroy them in the name of Jesus. Amen!

CHAPTER EIGHT

WANT PEACE, PREPARE FOR WAR!

I've been in ministry for some twenty plus years. I have the education to be able to counsel people who are hurting. Let me say that many of those who sit in our churches haven't got it together as they appear to. I mean we have become professional mask wearers. We can act like everything is OKAY! We know just how to respond to the altar calls. We have specialized in giving good testimonies. Just think about this for a moment. If your reading this book, you've gotten this far and were honest with yourself, even you have learned the proper responses to mask how you really feel.

The church that is suppose to be a place where you receive hope, healing and a peace of mind has become a cesspool of hurting, confused, bewildered and puzzled people who are dying inside and don't know how to release their nightmares. We have become specialists in hiding what we really think, what we really feel, and how we are really hurting. We sit week after week listening to a man of God who is telling us about heaven, hell and prosperity. While we are listening we never receive the spiritual medicine from the Lord that could immediately stop our hemorrhaging and aching heart. Every week people enter the doors of the church and leave the same way they came in...empty, hollow, hurting and confused. All the while we preach our sermons and scream out our messages that probably were not the result of prayer. They come from the latest "seeker friendly" book we bought entitled *"101 Sermons That Will Motivate the Pew."*

We cry we want more; more of God, more money and more knowledge. The truth is that we really don't need more. We need to use what we have already received. There's enough God in you right now to supply everything else you will ever need. Just stop searching and start realizing that the warfare is not to gain, but to give.

Want peace, prepare for war. The prosperity message, in my opinion, has gotten out of hand. There is no balance to the sowing and reaping message. People are leaving our services wondering why they keep giving. They wonder why they have to reach for change, but those who are suppose to be our examples never do. If we don't come to some kind of middle ground from the pulpit to the pew we are going to topple out of control. Warfare that's going to make a difference will be the warfare over your mind.

I want to share something with you at this point in my book. It's July 7, 2004, and I'm sitting on an airplane flying to Dallas to preach. We just finished a youth camp called "Beach Invasion." There were around 130 youth at this camp, and I began to minister for three nights on...well let me break it down for you.

Tuesday night I spoke to the youth about Gilgal. When Joshua was about to move into the promise land his first battle was going to be Jericho. There was no need for Joshua and the children of Israel to bother fighting Jericho until they stopped at Gilgal. They had to circumcise those who grew up in the wilderness and hadn't been marked with the covenant markings of circumcision. Now, here's a thought, why did they stop what God never told them to stop? When you live in a place called wilderness you tend to become lazy of the truths that keep you marked for blessing. It's called religion. They became bitter and hurt with God, and the reason they were not living in their promise position was not God's fault but theirs. Are you blaming God when in reality it's your fault? Now pace your anger! They stopped the process of change and growth and began to live life on what we like to call going through the motions. They were after all God's chosen, they were indisputably God's people, yet they lacked the passion to keep there distinction. Have you done the same?

"So Joshua made flint knives for himself, and circumcised the sons of Israel at the hill of the foreskins. And this is the reason why Joshua circumcised them: All the people who came out of Egypt who were males, all the men of war, had died in the wilderness on the way, after they had come out of Egypt. For all the people who came out had been circumcised, but all the people born in the wilderness, on the way as they came out of Egypt, had not been circumcised." Joshua 5:3-5 NKJV

I expressed to these youth that they needed to cut off those things that had been hurting them. My heart began to sink as I kept ministering and dealing with subjects such as, bitterness, pain, molestation and parental abuse... to see that most of these youth were being affected by what I was saying. The numbers are staggering; around 80 percent of those youth stood and confessed that they needed to cut off what had been causing them pain.

> **BEHIND EVERY MESSED UP TEENAGER THERE IS USUALLY A MESSED UP PARENT!**

Favor Key: "Your pain today not dealt with, becomes your poison tomorrow."

Wednesday night we moved to Jericho. Now, Jericho represents the walls we built while we were being hurt.

"Now Jericho was securely shut up because of the children of Israel; none went out, and none came in." Joshua 6:1 NKJV

We all have been hurt and built walls around those hurts. It's easy to build them! Jericho was tightly shut up, and no one went out and no one came in. As long as those walls are up no one can really love you and you can't really love someone else. Walls inhibit our ability to emotionally mature. Watching once again the hands that went up and the tears that fell from those teenagers' faces was heart wrenching. These are kids from the ages of 12 to 19. They should not have to deal with pain, betrayal, loneliness and bitterness.

Behind every messed up teenager is a messed up parent. What does this hurting generation of teenagers do with all that pain? They build walls! Nothing gets out and nothing gets in. How about you, have you built walls around your heart? Are you a woman who has been hurt by abuse or betrayal? Are you a person who has been molested as a child? Are you a single mother who has been left by your spouse to raise the kids all by yourself? Most likely you have built walls around your heart. Pain, bitterness and defeat can't get out, and you will not let God, His minister or His people in.

Do what the majority of those teenagers at camp did, and tear down those walls. Do it right now. Tear down:
- Walls of anger...

WANT PEACE, PREPARE FOR WAR

- Walls of sexual abuse…
- Walls of deceit…
- Walls of bitterness…
- Walls of divorce…

How are they going to fall? **By faith**! You must believe that when you break down those walls God will do the rest. Do what you can, and God will do what you can't! Give your heart permission to be healed. Do it right now! Lay a hand over your heart and say this out loud, HEART BE HEALED. Say it three times.

Did you feel that? God just entered behind the walls that you have had shut up in your life for years.
One more thing, as long as you keep those doors or walls closed it gives the enemy a place to hide. No matter what you try to do Satan will always have a place to enter your season and bring up stuff in your past to destroy what God is doing in your present.

Warfare is necessary. Warfare can only exist when two parties want the same thing. There will never be secure peace unless you have the strength to fight the enemy that is trying to break up your peace. Want peace, prepare for war. This is why I believe that a strong military in our country guarantees certain peace. When you deplete your strength you give your enemies hope to conquer. We, as believers, need to maintain a good spiritual military front. We need to let the devil know that if he wants us, he's going to have to fight us. There are certain things that must be known in every war.

First, there must be a **TARGET.**

Without a target, we don't know what to shoot at. The enemy has a target, and that target is not you as much as what is in you. Satan isn't really after you, but what you've been purposed to do for the Lord. Your purpose and your anointing to fulfill that purpose is hells number one target. The more a person is filled with purpose the more likely he or she will become a target. Warfare always surrounds the birth of a miracle. Opposition is merely a signal that you are where you are suppose to be... doing what you are suppose to be doing! You will always bring out the beasts of hell when you are full of the Holy Spirit. The word full means to be controlled by a greater power or to be under the influence of another force or person. In Acts chapter two the hundred twenty were all filled with the Holy Spirit. They were empowered, or controlled by a greater force. What Peter couldn't get walking three years with Jesus; he received in a day when he was filled with the Holy Spirit. This was the very reason that Jesus instructed all His followers to go and wait until they have been endued with power! You can't win on your own strength; you're going to need this endowment. When this takes place get ready, you're about to become Satan's number one target. What's in you is dangerous! Get excited when you see trouble all around you. You are now Satan's target, but if your Satan's target you're also God's weapon.

SECOND, THERE MUST **BE TIMING**.

Timing is very important. When did the enemy go after Jesus in Luke chapter three verse twenty-one through twenty-two? Right after Jesus receives a Word from the God. When Jesus came up out of the Jordan, the heavens opened, a dove ascended and a voice was spoke, identifying who He was, and what He was suppose to do. At what season can you expect great attack? Expect attack when you have just come through some great victory.

Timing plays an important role for both sides. Not only do you have to understand the timing of an attack. You need to also know when to take steps toward your purpose. Abilities and talents mean nothing out of timing. You can be the most gifted for a certain position, but step out of timing and miss your chance. Timing is very important to winning in warfare. Attack to soon and you can lose!

THIRD, THERE MUST BE PLACE TO FIGHT. **(TURF)**

For a battle to exist there must be a battlefield. On what battlefield can you expect the enemy to attack? Usually in the place where you are least likely to find help...when you are alone...when you are down or depressed...when someone has offended you or hurt you... when you've been let down by someone you trusted. The enemy loves to wait for you to be in the wilderness of your life, and when you think things can't get worse they usually do. When did Satan attack Jesus after His baptism? Forty days later, after He hadn't eaten and was hungry in the wilderness. Satan tried to get Jesus to submit to His humanity instead of Him acting on God's Word. The best place to win a battle, in my opinion, is on the enemy's own battlefield. Imagine what kind of victory has taken place when we beat the enemy on his own turf. This is exactly what Jesus did in Luke Chapter four verse one.

FOURTH, THERE MUST BE A **STRATEGY.**

The enemy will pour it on at your weakest moment. You'll be tested from above and tempted from within. The strategy will always be
- To discourage you…
- To disappoint you…
- To distract you…
- To derail you…
- To delay your harvest…

You must hold on… However long it has taken for victory is a clue to how big your harvest and spoils are. Paul said when you have done all you can, just stand! Don't give the enemy an inch. When you seem to have lost the ability to attack then just stand still and see the salvation of the Lord. Don't give up any ground. In every battle there is usually a victory. You and I have already won. There use to be this saying "I'm in it to win it."
WANT PEACE, PREPARE FOR WAR

Well I'm not in it to win it, because I've already won it. Stand, fight and win!

Want peace, prepare for war. Let me close this chapter with this key. Never, ever, ever go to war where there are no spoils. Remember, you are entitled to the wealth of every enemy that you conquer. Behind every giant there is a bag full of blessings. Don't go to war where there are no bags of blessings.

"(For the weapons of our warfare are not carnal, but mighty through God to the pulling down of strong holds;") 2 Corinthians 10:4 KJV

"This charge I commit unto thee, son Timothy, according to the prophecies which went before on thee, that thou by them might war a good warfare; Holding faith, and a good conscience; which some having put away concerning faith have made shipwreck."
1 Timothy 1:18-19 KJV

CHAPTER NINE

HOW TO SURVIVE THE WHIRLWIND

"They sow the wind, and reap the whirlwind."
Hosea 8:7 NKJV

My spiritual father, Dr. Mike Murdock, was mentoring me one afternoon and said with great conviction; **"Decisions decide your wealth."** I began to meditate on what Dr. Mike said. I realized in my meditation that we all make decisions everyday. Good ones and bad ones. Our decisions are either promoting us or demoting us. I know that I mentioned the same statement about decisions early in this manuscript. It is an important process to understanding the law of failure in sin. Most of us really don't have a major problem. The only problem we face is a decision problem... We can fix a lot of fragmented pieces of our life just by taking the time necessary to make a good decision.

John 6:12 says *"...Gather up the fragments that remain, that nothing be lost."*

Pick up the fragmented pieces so that none is lost. Life is made up of fragmented pieces. We have all experienced the power of fragmented decisions. Fragmented is to be broken off the whole.

.

The word "fragmented" in Webster's Dictionary is defined as: *"a part broken away from a whole; broken piece, a detached, isolated, or incomplete part. The part that exists of a literary or other worked left unfinished."* ©1995 Zane Publishing, Inc.   ©1994, 1991, 1988 Simon & Schuster, Inc.

The world has become a fragmented mess. We see dysfunctional families everywhere. I once read a survey years ago that stated, "There are approximately two hundred million marriages a year…Out of them one hundred, one million and seventy divorce." That's staggering to me. Mind you, I read this survey in the 80's… Today, I'm sure it's worse! Our families and our homes are being torn apart by fragmented relationships. People have lost the true meaning to what it means to make a commitment. If you stop liking your spouse trade them for another one seems to be the practice today! Love isn't a feeling; love is a decision. Reading newspapers and magazines makes it obvious that the population is under a different kind of value system. The main theme today is when you stop liking it trade it, get rid of it and dispose of it! This mentality has bled over into the church. If you don't like what's going on LEAVE! Just make the same move as the sheep that wander from church to church.

No wonder our churches are in pieces. The way the family goes, so goes the church! Let me interject here what I am accustomed to saying to those who want to seek money and fame.

- Money can buy you a house, but it can't buy you a home.
- Money can buy you stuff, but it can't buy you happiness.
- Money can do a lot of things, but it can't buy you peace of mind.

Only Jesus can do that! The Word declares that in His presence there is fullness of joy. Joy and peace can only survive in the atmosphere of the Lord Jesus. There can be no wholeness without His peace. How many times has someone you've known walked away from their life of wholeness and moved into a life that is fragmented and broken? What was the result? Remember, it was probably their decision that plummeted them into their dysfunction and they became detached. They begin to isolate themselves from anyone who can give them good counsel to promote them out of their depression. *Why is it, that when we as people are hurting or betrayed we immediately want to isolate and become detached?* I believe that it is because it is easier to have a pity party and feel sorry about yourself while you're alone. Pity parties are the worst parties. Usually, you are the only one at your pity party. This is where the enemy can do his best work of deception. It's in the dark closest of failure that Satan can build his stronghold of defeat, distraction and discouragement. There are so many fragmented pieces, and they are all pointing at you now. Each fragmented piece is screaming out to your spirit about all the mistakes and bad decisions you have made.

We see and experience broken fragmented pieces in lives every day. Have you ever sat and stared into space and realized that your life has been fragmented, broken and detached? Your once pristine life is now a literal mess... What troubles you even deeper, is that this mess was caused by your own actions and your own decisions! You are now sitting in the middle of a whirlwind you caused. Trouble has surrounded you on all sides. What is the answer? First, you must face that you are flawed. You made the decisions that caused your once picture perfect world to be disrupted. Trying to pin your problems on everyone and everything around you will only slow down the process of getting out of what's troubling you.

FRAGMENTED:
We see fragmented things all around us... from the news on television to the crisis in other countries. We see them in our homes, at our work places, in our immediate family and all around us the world has been fragmented. **When was the last time you actually experienced real peace**?

If you are experiencing depression or discouragement and feel like withdrawing from those around you, ***don't!*** Isolation is not healthy. We need each other! We need to seek godly counsel and obey that counsel. ***Healing is scheduled for you***! Just don't quit! Don't give into hiding and detaching yourself from those who care about you. I know that when you are hurting, and the result of your pain was decided by your own actions, it's hard. It's embarrassing to be around other people. Let me encourage you to do what is good for you, not what you feel is good. No one has ever lived through these moments without someone beside them cheering them on; encouraging them; letting them know that God is comfortable with their flaws and bad decisions. Just don't give up! Stay focused on the Lord. He's not giving up on you so don't give up on you either.

What causes the whirlwind?

IGNORANCE:
"Because they hated knowledge and did not choose the fear of the LORD." Proverbs 1:29 NKJV

Ignorance is the most common weapon against those who are willing to do better. It's not that people want to see trouble and experience pain. I can't for one moment believe that people who are in a whirlwind, got up and decided they wanted to experience life through the whirlwind of pain, disappointments and depression. It's not what you know that's hurting you; it's what you don't know. *Knowledge is more powerful than gold.*

You don't have to look far or long to find ignorance... if

you are like me, you can probably look in the mirror of your past and find where you made many bad decisions because of ignorance. Ignorance doesn't mean you're stupid. I was preaching in a service and mentioned that the reason we are so defeated in the body of Christ is because we are ignorant of what we have been promised by God. A person came to me afterwards and rebuked me. Their comment to me was that you shouldn't call people stupid. My comment was, "I didn't call anyone stupid... I called them ignorant." Stupid means you can't learn... no matter how hard you try, you just don't get it. **Ignorance** is that you refuse to learn. Ignorance is when you have the ability to gather the information necessary to shorten your season of trouble and lack, but you simply refuse to pursue it. The church is full of ignorant people.

DISOBEDIENCE:
"Let no one deceive you with empty words, for because of these things the wrath of God comes upon the sons of disobedience. Therefore do not be partakers with them."
Ephesians 5:6-7 NKJV

God will never take you past your last act of disobedience. When God gives us an instruction he has a plan of promotion in mind. His instruction is a test. Your willingness to obey is proof you are in line with what the Lord desires for your life as well as those around you.
__The difference between seasons in your life is an INSTRUCTION...__

When God wanted to change Noah's season and rescue him from a major whirlwind, or hurricane, God gave him an instruction.

"And God said to Noah, "The end of all flesh has come before Me, for the earth is filled with violence through them; and behold, I will destroy them with the earth. Make yourself an ark..." Genesis 6:13-14 NKJV

Most of God's instructions will seem illogical but not impossible. God's instructions will never fit into your intellectual way of thinking. In Noah's situation, God was about to destroy mankind because of man's wickedness, yet, God had to spare someone to carry on the bloodline of Adam so that He could implement his plan of redemption.

Noah found favor in the sight of the Lord. What was it about Noah that caught the interest of God? Noah's name means quiet, peaceful, to settle down. Noah was comfortable with not being in the crowd. Noah was a man who was at peace with himself... he didn't need to do what everyone was doing. The times were appalling as man was walking in every kind of wickedness.

"Because of these things the wrath of God is coming upon the sons of disobedience." Colossians 3:6 NKJV

"When the whirlwind passes by, the wicked is no more, but the righteous has an everlasting foundation." Proverbs 10:25 NKJV

What do you do when you've sown to the wind and you have reaped the whirlwind?

I can't help but notice in my own life how many stupid decisions I have made through the years. Decisions I make today create the consequences I will face tomorrow. Many times in our lives we blame the enemy for what's going on around us. We blame the devil when in reality the devil wasn't our problem.

What do you do? You do what Eve did! You pick up the fragmented pieces...*Genesis 4:25* gives us the example on how to survive the whirlwind.

Imagine what must have gone through Eve's mind... She was promised a seed... She gave birth to two sons, Cain and Abel. Watching them grow up... waiting for her seed to deliver her from what they did wrong. All of the sudden, in one day her whole life is affected by the whirlwind. Cain rises up against Abel and kills him. God enters the scene, curses Cain, exiles him to the hills and curses his linage. Eve's once unspoiled life was now in an upheaval, and she stands on the rock of pain and confusion. I can't imagine what it must be like to lose a child much less two. I would have fallen in the dirt and cried until there were no tears left in me. Eve probably fell on her rock of desperation and pain crying and sobbing with all her might. Every muscle in her body ached with the brokenness of her heart for her children. She realized that she was reaping what she sowed. What does she do on the rock of pain, hurt and disappointment? She doesn't stay there. She turns her rock of pain into a rock of determination. After all God did promise her a seed. Why not do what Eve did instead of sitting in your hurt and pain?

"And Adam knew his wife again, and she bore a son and named him Seth." Genesis 4:25 NKJV

Eve was willing to get up out of her problem and try one more time. Adam knew Eve again; again mind you! Eve tried one more time. This time she conceives and has a son named Seth, and Seth has a son named Enosh. Enosh means that men began to call on the name of the Lord.

"And as for Seth, to him also a son was born; and he named him Enosh. Then men began to call on the name of the LORD." Genesis 4:26 NKJV

Don't panic in the whirlwind. You may have to live through the consequences of a bad decision, but the promise that was given will keep you alive until it is fulfilled. Don't lose sight of His promise. The Lord is still in control even in the whirlwind.

"The LORD hath his way in the whirlwind and in the storm, and the clouds are the dust of his feet." Nahum 1:3 KJV

Never give in to your mistake! We all make bad

decisions, and we all have had to pay for them. You can survive your whirlwind. God is not going to destroy you as along as you keep getting up and fighting. Struggle is proof that sin hasn't conquered you. Pride is not going to be an easy opponent. I am convinced that Goliath wasn't David's test. Goliath died too easy. Anything that dies that easy isn't what is standing between you and your promotion. I believe that Saul was the real test. David had to out last King Saul. He had to learn how to survive before he would arrive as King. You and I are going to have to do the same. Don't let yesterday's failure become today's defeat. The mercies of the Lord are new every morning.

"It is of the LORD's mercies that we are not consumed, because his compassions fail not. They are new every morning: great is thy faithfulness."
Lamentations 3:22-23 KJV

DR. JERRY A. GRILLO, JR.

CHAPTER TEN

EVERYBODY WANTS TO GO TO HEAVEN BUT NOBODY WANTS TO DIE!

*"But Jesus answered them, saying, "The hour has come that the Son of Man should be glorified. Most assuredly, I say to you, unless a grain of wheat falls into the ground and dies, it remains alone; but if it dies, it produces much grain. He who loves his life will lose it, and he who hates his life in this world will keep it for eternal life. If anyone serves Me, let him follow Me; and where I am, there My servant will be also. If anyone **serves me, him My** Father will honor. "Now My soul is troubled, and what shall I say? 'Father, save Me from this hour'? But for this purpose I came to this hour."* John 12:23-27 NKJV

We live in such a cynical and cruel world. We try hard not to become critical and cynical toward those around us. It's easy for me to become angry and bitter when I look around me and see the world prospering and advancing in their lives and careers and not adhering to the laws of God.

Watching television doesn't help either. It is rampant with get rich quick programs and infomercials. We sit in our lounge chairs with a bowl of popcorn and a diet coke dreaming of bigger and better things. Bigger houses, bigger cars and bigger checking accounts, but the only thing growing bigger is our stomach! Then our government isn't helping either with the lottery popping up everywhere. People are doing everything they can to get it quick and easy.

The people of the 21st century have become a people who desire to live the life of convenience. We expect to receive the fullness of what life has to offer, and never stop to ponder what the price tag for it is. The very freedom we live in had a price tag placed upon it. Men fought and died for this freedom. I become outraged when I sit and watch the television and see people stomping and burning our flag. I sit there with disdain for those people who, in stupidity, desecrate the very thing that bought them the right to stomp on it. Anything worth having always comes with a cost.

It cost what it cost and it isn't going on sale. If you want to walk in courage it will cost you. Want freedom? It will cost you. Want prosperity? It will cost you. We need to understand that everything in life that's worth having is going to cost something.

Salvation isn't free. I can't stand it when preachers say salvations free. Free! Have we forgotten what God did for us so that we could become saved? Someone had to pay for our sins and that person was Jesus. So how can salvation be free?

There's life after the cross. What do we do after we accept the cross and the man on the cross? Do we just sit at the cross and stare at its empty beams? I think not! We must move beyond the cross to the empty tomb, past the tomb to a walk of love, faith, power and increase. Learn to kill the flesh. Here's a thought, while we're standing at the foot of the cross why not go ahead and have another crucifixion...nail your flesh to the cross. Kill it good and dead.

God will schedule death on every promise He makes. David Wilkerson preached a message years ago entitled "Death of a Promise." Why does God schedule death you may ask? First, let's look at some scriptural examples.

God promised Abraham a son, but He waited until Sarah, Abraham's wife, had a dried up womb. Abraham's seed within him was almost dead. Then, when Abraham is 99 years old, God brings the promise, a son named Isaac. Mind you after the promise died.

David didn't become king the day he was anointed by the prophet Samuel. What he thought would have happened immediately would take years to manifest. Now he had to live out the process to become king... David had to kill a giant... David had to run from Saul... David had to live in caves with thieves and robbers... David had to act like a mad man and hide in the enemy's camp. What appeared to be impossible and dead didn't come about until God was ready to bring it to fulfillment. Every promise has a sentence of death scheduled to it. God is developing your faith to trust Him and Him alone. When the promise does arrive you'll only have God to praise.

QUIT TRYING TO KEEP ALIVE WHAT GOD'S BEEN TRYING TO KILL!

WHAT DO I DO WHILE I WAIT?

"Yet, looking unto the promise of God, he (Abraham) wavered not through unbelief, but waxed strong through faith, giving glory to God." Romans 4:20 NKJV

First, we must do what Abraham did. We must not waver in believing God for the promise. God has declared in His Word that He is not a man that He would tell a lie. If God said it, then we must believe it is on the way.

Faith is not receiving what God said; faith believes that you will receive what God said. You must understand that time is not your enemy or your problem. Time is what takes place after you've been given a promise. God will not let you die until He has made good what He said.

To waver is to show doubt or indecision… to swing or sway one way or another. Abraham didn't waver. He stayed true and constant in his belief that God was able to do what He said He would do. Most of us do not receive the promise because we do not continue with Christ. We quit the moment we are hurt or offended…the moment we didn't receive what we thought we ought to have received in the time frame we deemed we should have received it.

That's right; we just stop doing what we should and start doing what we shouldn't. We just quit. We stop going to church, stop paying our tithes, stop believing for the miracle and start complaining about the moments.

We just can't stand to be put on hold, and when we are we just quit.

If it dies it multiples!

Death assigned to a seed gives the seed the ingredients it needs to become something greater. A seed that doesn't die can't produce anything, but a seed that is buried and dies produces what you and I call a harvest. Many are fed and taken care of through the process of death. Death is necessary for the seed to resurrect into something much greater.

WAIT THERE'S MORE…

Second, you must change your view of what is taking place when you are waiting for your promised harvest.

Some view the time as failure; others simply believe they missed God. The one thing we all have in common is that we have all made mistakes and have failed, but our view of failure helps us understand the waiting process for our promise.

Failure is truths apprenticeship. Failure is the only place where we can learn what not to do in certain situations. It's what you do after you have made a mistake that determines if you are a failure.

Failure will better change us into the image of God. It's our mistakes that cause us to understand the mercies of God. Mary Magdalene understood the mercies of God when Jesus rescued her from her accusers.

If you had the privilege to have watched the "Passion of the Christ" by Mel Gibson, you will remember the scene with Mary Magdalene when she was thrown at Jesus' feet? She kept her head in the dirt waiting for the rocks of guilt and shame to smash into her. After all, she was caught in the very act of her sin. She was by all rights guilty, and the law was clear, she must be stoned. Here she waits at His feet, never looking at Jesus but waiting. She waited for the rocks of her accusers to hit her. Why should this man Jesus treat her any other way than the way any other man has ever treated her?

Isn't it crazy, God uses a man to restore her, and it was men that were taking advantage of her? God used the very thing that was destroying her to restore her… A **MAN**! Grant it, Jesus wasn't going to be like any other men. He was going to throw a rock, but his rock was the **ROCK OF SALVATION!**

It cost what it cost… Stop trying to get what the Lord has on the clearance rack of some dead church. What the Lord has for us is going to cost us. Heaven is not free! Salvation isn't free either. Don't think for one moment that salvation was free. When you develop this mentality you cheapen the cost of your freedom. Someone had to pay in order for you and me to be free. Grant it you didn't pay, but someone did. Remember the old song… *I owed a debt I could not pay; Jesus paid a debt he did not owe.*

What heaven has for us is going to cost us. Let's stop trying to cheapen heaven's wealth. Want a harvest, then guess what, you're going to have to sow. Want healing, you're going to have to confess and believe for your healing. Want protection from God, your going to have to tithe. Want friendship, you're going to have to be a friend. There is a price for everything you want.

I know that you're going to raise the bar and jump to the next season of your life. Let those things die that need to die so that you can expect a resurrection in your life.

CONCLUSION

I cannot express what a joy it was for me to be able to write this book, "Sin Is Not Your Problem." I wrote this book for those who struggle day to day, trying to conquer a life of sin and in the end seem to be losing the struggle.

It's easy to begin to feel the frustrations of warfare. They call it battle fatigue. When fatigue sets in, faith goes out. There is always going to be frustrations when we enter into a battle assuming that if we win we have defeated the culprit that is causing me to sin. When we discover that every time I fight sin, I seem to win some and lose some... My failures are always more damaging to me than my victories are over the sin.

I set out to explain why, when I've done all I can do to help someone who is struggling with a certain sin; such as addiction, lust, bitterness, disobedience, homosexuality and so many others, yet they still keep sinning. There was so many years that I accepted the traditional excuse that these people really didn't want to stop sinning. I have now come to the conclusion that this is not all true. I've been with these people... prayed with them... counseled them! They weren't evil or mean spirited. They were genuine in there desire to stop what the enemy had placed in their life as a stronghold. I know that even some of them prayed daily. They read their Word daily and in the end would seem to give in to what they thought they were destroying in their prayer closet.

I realized that they were fighting the consequence and not

the cause. Everything that God made has a cause and effect relationship. When we don't discover the cause, we will always have the same effect. For instance, if we drink water, we will eventually have to expel that water. To every action there is a greater or equal reaction. Sin is the reaction of a deeper demon. I know that if you took the time to study this book and let the spirit of this book sink in, you will be on your way to total domination over the sin that has so easily beset you.

Let me add. I didn't write this book as some great theologian or for someone to discuss with me the plurality of life. I wrote this book as a help tool to those who want to walk free from their sin life. I don't have all the answers... I do believe that this manuscript is going to be a great source to start you on your way to victory. Remember, there is no one great key to escaping the darkness of a bad decision. We all must submit to the mercies of God. However, we can accumulate the necessary knowledge so that we don't have to keep repeating the same mistake. The purpose of this book is to help you stop repeating what you want to walk in victory over.

I do appreciate you taking the time to read this book. If you believe that it helped you, and you know it will help someone you know, feel free to order more at a wholesale discount. Email me and let me know that you are buying this book as a seed to help others and I will discount it to help you sow.

I love you dearly; you matter to this ministry and you matter to me greatly. I look forward to being in your area soon. Until then, walk in the F.O.G. (Favor of God)

Dr. Jerry A. Grillo, Jr.

WHAT OTHERS ARE SAYING ABOUT
DR. JERRY A. GRILLO

Bishop Jerry Grillo lives what he teaches. It has been my privilege to be his personal friend for a number of years. He is a living example of a victorious leader. His church is a victorious church. If you can't succeed under this man of God you can't succeed anywhere. His revelation is life's fresh air in a stagnant world. He is one of the happiest and most exciting leaders I have known through my thirty-eight years of world evangelism. It is my privilege to recommend any book he has written.

> Dr. Mike Murdock
> The Wisdom Center
> Dallas, TX.

Bishop Jerry Grillo is truly a gift from God to my life. I love his passion, his purity and his painstaking commitment to purpose. It is very obvious that he loves the God he preaches to us about. Should you ever have the privilege of peaking into this life, you would know without a doubt he's one of God's favorite. Bishop Grillo, what a wonderful refreshing, what a wonderful friend!

> Pastor Sheryl Brady
> Sheryl Brady Ministries
> Raleigh NC.

A spiritual physician that I was privileged to meet some time ago was Bishop Jerry Grillo, the author of this powerful book. When I met the man, I knew it was more than just a casual acquaintance – it was a divine appointment. There are many men of ministry that we meet down through the course of destiny, but not everyone you encounter has the energy of greatness that precedes their introduction or conversation. To meet the man in person, you immediately recognize that he is more than just a man with another message, but he is one who carries the mantle of favor upon his life – appointed and anointed for this season. He is a husband, a father, a pastor, teacher, and a scribe with a prescription to challenge you from poverty to prosperity, from fear to faith and from failure into favor.

Bishop Joby Brady
The River Fellowship, Inc
Raleigh, NC

If you have been looking for a shining light to cut through the fog of doubt and shine forth the F.O.G. (favor of God), you have found it. These series of manuscripts are some of the most powerful teachings on favor that are in the Christian world today. Bishop Jerry Grillo, I believe is one of the premier voices to this generation... Get ready; the chains of doubt, poverty and lack are about to be broken off your life.

Pastor Clint Brown
Faith World Center
Orlando, FL.

I count it a blessing and a privilege to call Bishop Grillo my friend. He has been a source of inspiration and encouragement to my life, and I know he will do the same for you. I am excited for you as you embark on a new path of revelation and truths...

Dr. H. Michael Chitwood
"The Authority"

If you haven't heard Bishop Jerry Grillo preach on favor you have missed one of the nation's best...

Bishop Don Meares
Evangel Cathedral
Upper Marlboro MD

Decision Page

May I Invite You To Make Jesus Christ The Lord Of Your Life?

The Bible says, *"That if you will confess with your mouth the Lord Jesus, and will believe in your heart that God raised Him from the dead, you will be saved. For with the heart man believes unto righteousness; and with the mouth confession is made for salvation."* Romans 10:9,10

Pray this prayer with me today:
"Dear Jesus, I believe that you died for me and rose again on the third day. I confess to you that I am a sinner. I need your love and forgiveness. Come into my life, forgive my sins and give me eternal life. I confess you now as my Lord. Thank you for my salvation! I walk in your peace and joy from this day forward. Amen!"

Signed_____

Date _____

[Mail this in to Dr. Grillo]

☐ *Yes, Dr. Jerry! I made a decision to accept Christ as my personal Savior today, and I would like to placed on your mailing list.*

*Name*_____

*Address*_____

*City*_____

State _____ *Zip* _____ *Phone*_____

*Birth Date*_____

FOGZONE MINISTRIES
P.O. Box 3707, Hickory N.C. 28603
828.325.4773 Fax: 828.325.4877 www.fogzone.net

Will You Become A Favored Champion Partner?

"What You Connect To You Will Eventually Become."

Church Meetings - Multitudes are ministered to in crusades and seminars throughout America in "The Favor Conferences." Bishop's heart is for the Senior Pastors.

Books and Literature – Dr. Grillo has written over eight books… with over 20 book ideas to be completed. "Daddy God" is given to many around the nation as a seed book. Bishop's heart is to reach out to those in prisons and to accommodate those who are hurting; he sows "Daddy God" to a majority of Prison Ministries around the nation.

Videos and Tapes – Thousands are listening to Bishop all over the country, through his videos and tape ministry. He has over 40 series to offer the Body of Christ.

Missionary Ministry – Dr. Grillo is dedicated to outreach. His outreach ministry feeds cloths and ministers to thousands each year. It is the passion of Fogzone Ministry to help build outreach ministries all over the nation.

Television and Radio – The Favor message is being aired all over the nation. Bishop has appeared on **TBN**, **The Harvest Show, Lesea Broadcasting**, **WBTV 49** Augusta GA., **WATV 57** Atlanta GA, and so many more. Bishop's ministry is changing millions. "**FAVOR KEYS**," seen each week on the UPN Network, reaches 6.8 million people.

MADE POSSIBLE BY OUR MONTHLY FAVORED CHAMPION PARTNERS.

FAVORED PARTNERSHIP PLAN

Dear Favored Partner,

God has brought us together... When we get involved with God's plans, He will get involved with our plans. To accomplish any vision it takes **partnership**...It takes people like you and me coming together to accomplish the plan of God.

WILL YOU BECOME ONE OF MY FAVORED PARTNERS TO HELP CARRY THE BLESSINGS OF GOD ACROSS THIS NATION?

In doing so there are three major harvests that you are going to experience...

1. *Harvest of Supernatural Favor*
2. *Harvest for Financial Increase*
3. *Harvest for Family Restoration*

Sit down and write the first check by faith, if God doesn't increase you in the next months you are not obligated to sow the rest.

Yes, Dr. Grillo, I want to be one of your monthly partners... I am coming into agreement with you right now for my **THREE MIRACLE HARVEST'S**.

Thank you,

Dr. Jerry A. Grillo, Jr.

PARTNERSHIP PLAN:

_____**300 Favored Champion Partner**: Yes, Dr. Grillo I want to be one of you Favored Champion Partners of $42.00 a month; involving my seed as one of the 300 who help Gideon conquer the enemy of lack.

_____**70 Favored Elders**: Yes, Dr. Grillo I want to be one of you 70 Favored Elders of $100.00 a month. I want to be one of those who will help lift your arms so that we can win over the enemy of fear and failure.

Name_____

Address_____

City _____State_____ Zip_ _____

Phone _____Email _____

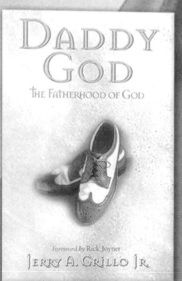

Get ready for the power of favor to increase everything you do. God is about to pour out His blessings on you and on those around you.

Weather Forecast for Your Future $9.99

The Weather forecast for your future is extreme F.O.G. the favor of God. Favor is the greatest gift God has given to man...learn how to activate the favor of God in your life.

God's Unwavering $9.99 Faithfulness

God will keep His covenant no matter what your circumstance. In this book, God's Unwavering Faithfulness, you will discover that God is faithful no matter what!

Dr. Jerry A. Grillo, Jr.

FILL OUT THIS FORM AND MAIL INTO FOGZONE MINISTRIES

Name: _____

Address: _____

City:_____State:_____ Zip:_____

Phone: _____

Credit Card#: _____

Exp. Date: _____Signature:_____

Visa   MasterCard   Discover   American Express

QTY	ITEM	AMT	TOTAL
	FINANCIAL FAVOR SYSTEM (with "40 Facts to Financial Favor")	$ 99.00	
	FAITH FACTOR	$ 49.00	
	SETBACKS INTO COMEBACKS	$29.00	
	DELIVER ME FROM ME	$29.00	
	HOW TO SURVIVE FAMINE	$15.00	
	EXTREME F.O.G.	$ 9.99	
	FAVOR MAKES NO SENSE	$ 9.99	
	DADDY GOD	$ 9.99	
	FAITHFULNESS OF GOD	$ 9.99	
	40 FACTS TO FINANCIAL FAVOR	$ 8.00	